THE HUMILITY
OF CHRIST

Marty Wooten

The Humility of Christ
The Foundation for Spiritual Growth

ISBN: 978-1-958723-56-2.

Cover book design: Toney Mulhollan.

Dr. Marty Wooten served in the ministry for more than thirty years and has been involved in teaching and preaching in many churches both nationally and internationally. He earned a BA in biblical studies, a Masters of Divinity, a Masters of Theology, and a Doctorate in Ministry. He now makes his home in Madisonville, Louisiana with his wife, Cathy. Marty and Cathy have three adult children, Cristen, Catherine, and Michael. This is Marty's latest book. His previous book, *Power in Weakness: Second Corinthians and the Ministry of Paul* is available at www.ipibooks.com.

ILLUMINATION
PUBLISHERS

www.ipibooks.com

TABLE OF CONTENTS

INTRODUCTION 1

Chapter One–   Facing The Man in The Mirror:
An Arduous Task...7

Chapter Two–   Our Nothingness before God..............................17

Chapter Three– Our "Success" and the Humility
of Christ...35

Chapter Four–   Humility: The Power Behind Faith
and Love 65

Chapter Five–   Suffering and Christ's Humility.........................75

Chapter Six–   Humility and Leadership....................................95

CONCLUSION 131

Introduction

Do nothing out of selfish ambition or vain conceit, but in humility consider others better than yourselves. Each of you should look not only to their own interests but also to the interests of others. Your attitude should be the same as that of Christ Jesus: Who being in very nature God, did not consider equality with God something to be grasped, but made himself nothing, taking the very nature of a servant being made in human likeness. And being found in appearance as a man, he humbled himself and became obedient to death—even death on a cross. Therefore God exalted him to the highest place and gave him the name that is above every name . . . (Philippians 2:3-9)

In a world driven by success, individualism, greed, and power, how is it possible to avoid selfish ambition and vain conceit, to view others and their interests better than our own, and still survive? And even if we achieve all of these great virtues mentioned in the text above, how is it possible to empty ourselves and follow Christ's example of "nothingness"?[1] How does the attitude of Christ change us so that we can achieve what seems so impossible—this depth of unity and love for one another?

---

[1] Other English translations render the phrase, *made himself nothing,* as, *he emptied himself.*

It is obvious looking at the world around us that people have difficulty resolving conflict, and loving and forgiving others, sadly even in the church. Paul penned the above quoted words to the church in Phillippi because they were having their own problems with disunity. Humility at this point in Paul's letter took the lead as the main virtue set forth for genuine unity and conflict resolution to occur. Paul admonishes the disciples to imitate the nothingness of Christ and stated, *"but in humility . . . do all of these things"* (2:3). He refers to Jesus as having *"humbled himself"* (2:7).

Humility is in the spotlight because without it Jesus could not have fulfilled his mission and we cannot fulfill ours. Yet, though critically foundational for following Christ, humility for many disciples of Christ is still illusive, not trusted as practical, or confused for weakness, lack of conviction, and an unwillingness to stand up for ourselves. Each of us needs to believe that the potential for humility is inside all of us, but unless we're willing to face and deal with our pride, arrogance, selfishness, greed, and whatever other sins inhibit the growth of humility, humility will remain dormant. Hopefully, throughout this book we can provide some insight into how humility can emerge above all of the challenges.

The idea of Jesus becoming *nothing* is a mysterious concept, yet offers us rich insight into the meaning of humility if we are willing to explore it. Jesus willingly gave up equality with God in order to enter history. In doing so, he descended into "nothingness" – defined as the act of becoming a man. As a result, God exalted him and gave the name above every name – that is, Christ's "somethingness," if you will. For a short time Jesus knew he was just another lowly carpenter's son, a human being, a "nothing" in the eyes of the world. His confidence, in spite of the challenges of his "nothingness" was a result of his conviction of the innate "somethingness" he had because of his relationship to the Father. He knew how to center himself on that reality in order to keep his focus.

Jesus was fully aware of his destiny to suffer and die for the sins of the world. Yet, he was able to keep his commitment and inner resolve to complete the task. How? He humbled himself, which shows humility not as a weakness, but the central part of a disciple's armor against the selfishness, insensitivity, and greed of our sinful natures. It plugs us into a perspective which enables us to rise above our present trials and rejoice at the anticipated victories which lay ahead. The importance of a correct perspective will be discussed in chapter one.

The writer of the book of Hebrews states, *"Let us fix our eyes on Jesus, the author and perfecter of our faith, who for the joy set before him endured the cross, scorning its shame, and sat down at the right hand of the throne of God."* (HEBREWS 12:2) If our hope is truly a living hope as Peter describes it in 1 Peter 1:3, rather than just wishful thinking, then we have the opportunity to embrace the same emotions during our trials as we will have at our exaltation. James said, *"Consider it pure joy when you encounter trials of many kinds."* (JAMES 1:3) That's impossible unless we are convinced that our trials are to prepare us for our ultimate exaltation in heaven. This conviction is why Jesus was victorious.

Unfortunately, humility has not received much attention from Christian writers overall. Yet, it is the most basic virtue necessary to following Christ and determines our ability to embrace truth, knowledge about God, and the power to live an obedient life. It is a difficult topic to understand and even more difficult to apply to our lives.

Even with our best attempts at what we believe humility to be, it is usually not long before we take pride in our achievements and we are back to square one. In light of who Jesus proved himself to be, we can trust his acts of humility reflect a genuineness of heart and purpose. Not so with us unfortunately. It's much easier to learn to **act** humble than it is to **be** humble. A raging pride can be disguised easily with a facade of quietness, outward submission, and religiosity — a false humility as we call it. We all know how to act humble and selfless to hide our pride and self-centered agendas.

The Bible reminds us that God opposes the proud but gives grace to the humble. (JAMES 4:6) This makes the development and growth of humility in our lives serious business. Serious but possible if we are willing to press ahead in search of new insights and ways to move further towards the perfect humility of Christ. Truth-facing has a lot to do with our growth in humility — facing the truth about ourselves as God sees us and not how we want to see ourselves.

Every disciple has some measure of humility in order to be willing to follow Christ in the first place. The call, however, is to build on what we have already attained and to follow Jesus into the deepest levels of his humility. The real journey begins after our conversion. Regarding his desire to know Christ more fully, Paul said, *"Not that I have already obtained all this, or have already been made perfect, but I press on to take hold of that for which Christ Jesus took hold of me"* (PHILIPPIANS 3:12).

For humility to exist or to reach new heights, certain realities must be firmly in place. First, there must be the realization of our complete dependence on God both in the physical and spiritual realms, our frailty in comparison to God's power and the practical implications of that comparison. How we can deepen that recognition is a primary theme in this book.

Secondly, for our dependence on God to mature, God's view of us must be the standard for how we view ourselves. The objective truth must overcome the personal biases and fears we carry in regards to facing our true identity—what really makes us tick on the inside. The premise of this study is that the contents of the Bible, particularly those involving the life and teachings of Jesus Christ, are the standard by which a correct self-image can be ascertained. All of our opinions regarding who we think we are need consistent re-evaluation in light of God's Word.

Thirdly, what is also important is the interdependent relationship between humility and faith. It is difficult to know which comes first, faith or humility. Faith gives us the reason for our humility, yet humility is the seedbed for our faith. Humility creates an environment in which faith can blossom because humility involves a state of mind and perspective that frees the soul from self-serving interpretations of God's truths allowing us to properly evaluate the evidence for our faith. Without humility, there can be no faith in God and without faith there is no reason to be humble. In this book, we will not only look at examples of the humility of Christ, but we will also study some of the people Jesus commends as having great faith. It is there that we see the important relationship between humility and faith.

The quest for the humility of Christ is a never-ending journey—a journey with great rewards but also the greatest and most agonizing challenge of the Christian life. It takes courage, perseverance, and spiritual resiliency to follow someone who emptied himself and became nothing.

It is my prayer that this study provides some useful insight into the criticalness of humility to Christian living and the potential it has for leading us to the deeper truths of God. It is these truths which unleash the power of God in our lives.

handle their dirty feet. The religious and social caste system was firmly in place.

Jesus washing his disciples' feet was a complete and shocking social role reversal. He was the undisputed leader of the group, a man with the uncontested ability to perform miracles and healings never before heard of—he was God in the flesh. Deserving of having his own feet washed, the disciples had good cultural reasons to be shocked by Jesus' washing their feet. What would historically become one of the most memorable events in the ministry of Jesus initially left them in a confused daze. They were more concerned about the "somethingness" of their leader than they were about his mission of self-denial.

Notice the power of Jesus' identity-perspective over the social norms which typically would have determined his behavior.

Jesus knew that the Father had put all things under his power, and that he had come from God and was returning to God; so, he got up from the meal, took off his outer clothing, and wrapped a towel around his waist. After that, he poured water into a basin and began to wash his disciples' feet, drying them with the towel that was wrapped around him. (JOHN 13:3-5)

What Jesus "knew" is critical here. His identity as the Son of God was confirmed by the Father putting all things under his power. Though tempted to doubt his true identity, he knew who he was. His confidence in spite of the suffering of his humanity came from a deep understanding of where he came from and where he was going—*that he had come from God and was returning to God* . . . His time on earth was only a short stopover.

By focusing on his origin and ultimate destination Jesus was able to maintain an accurate identity-perspective and thus, withstand the atrocities of the present. People in search of an accurate definition of who they are, without the proper consideration of their origin, purpose, or final destination are excluding the most important pieces of the puzzle needed to bring clarity to the meaning of the present. Trying to live in the present without serious consideration of our past or future is nothing more than a meaningless existence in a purposeless single-dimensional vacuum.

An accurate view of ourselves is crucial to our confidence in our relationship with a loving and merciful God. For example, God has made it clear that if we are disciples of Christ our sins have been forgiven and we are saved. God promises that we do not need to fear death; we will live with him eternally. This is the objective truth.

In spite of this truth, some with a negative opinion of themselves do not feel secure in the possibility of that truth and have a haunting fear of death. These feelings are linked to a perceived state of being—they either see themselves as saved or not. Their identity-perspective—who they view themselves to be—is inaccurate and, therefore determines the course of life to be an insecure legalistic experience, rather than an experience of jubilant celebration of their new identity in Christ. Paul said, *"Therefore, there is no condemnation for those who **are** in Christ Jesus."* (ROMANS 8:1) [Emphasis mine]

The development of a true realization of God's view of us is a life-long process—that is to overcome the deficiencies in our subjective view of ourselves by opening our minds and hearts, as painful as that might be, to the light of God's objective truth and perfection.

The Nature of a Servant

Following the statement in PHILIPPIANS 2 about Jesus making himself nothing, there is a reference to Jesus, *taking the very nature of a servant.* The wording is important here. As we have already mentioned there is a big difference between serving outwardly and serving from the heart. Jesus didn't just decide to serve, but took the very nature of a servant. From that nature came his service.

One of the clearest definitions of the nature of a servant is recorded in LUKE 17:7-10:

> *Suppose one of you had a servant plowing or looking after the sheep. Would he say to the servant when he comes in from the field, 'Come along now and sit down to eat'? Would he not rather say, 'Prepare my supper, get yourself ready and wait on me while I eat and drink; after that you may eat and drink'? Would he thank the servant because he did what he was told to do? So, you also, when you have done everything you were told to do, should say, 'We are unworthy servants; we have only done our duty.'*

Servants were a typical part of the first century world and represented everything a Jew did not want to be. In fact, who in any century really wants to be someone else's servant? Because of the *nature* of the servant role Jesus makes it clear that a servant is not entitled to anything except a life of serving. Even the basic necessities of life—food and housing were determined by the subjective will of the master. If the master was decent, servants were fortunate. If he was evil, they were treated harshly. There was no legal system to hear their pleas, no housing authority, servants' advocacy associations, or legal rights for the elderly, and most of all, no clocking in and out. A servant was a servant 24/7. It was a thankless way of life. Granted there was an "upper crust" level of servanthood for the more privileged and educated servants who served in financial and administrative affairs for the wealthy. However, that is not the image or level of service Jesus had in mind.

It's not hard to get our minds around the idea of duty—something we are obligated to do—motivated by a sense of loyalty, patriotism, or contractual arrangement. But to view ourselves as unworthy while we fulfill our duty is at the heart of Jesus' challenge. The sense of entitlement in our hearts is what Jesus is going after. We might not mind serving from time to time in the church but it's much harder to be the only one serving. Often the more we serve the more we feel entitled to be relieved from our duties in a timely manner. A true servant was not entitled to any of these privileges and is expected to adapt to any situation regardless of the strenuosity of the task.

Christ: The Example of Living in Humility

The focus of this book involves more the practical implications of Christ's humility as defined in Philippians 2: 2-11 than the full contents of Philippians, except to point out an important foundational truth of the book. Philippians has traditionally been hailed as the "Epistle of Joy," because of its frequent references to joy in many different forms and derivatives, i.e. "joy," "rejoice," "joyful." Philippians is certainly unique in this respect.

However, this traditional view overlooks the real heart of the letter and the reason Paul speaks so often of joy. The number of references to "joy" in Philippians pale in comparison to the references to Jesus Christ. Paul uses every imaginable combination of title to reference Christ, i.e. Christ, Jesus, Jesus Christ, Christ Jesus, Lord Jesus Christ, and Spirit of Jesus Christ. He also uses Christ as the defining point in regards to many emotions, future events, and the purpose for his own life, i.e. "the day of Christ Jesus," "affection of Christ," and "for me to live is Christ."

That these references to Christ take prominence in Philippians is an important aspect of Paul's theology and speaks to the issue of spiritual identity. The experience of joy to which Paul refers is rooted in something other than what can be experienced merely in the physical realm. According to Paul it is only available in Christ, when one embraces a Christ who became nothing.

Joy can be experienced to some degree by the unbeliever but only when delusional or subjective interpretation of reality and spiritual truths takes place—a joy rooted in a spiritual mirage, a misguided hope, or attempt to find meaning and happiness in a temporal setting.

Therefore, even a joyous religious experience, in and of itself, doesn't make one a disciple of Christ. Jesus must become our "something" to the point that we are willing to follow him anywhere, even into his suffering and nothingness—the only barometer for what it means to be spiritually successful and genuinely joyful.

The joy of which Paul speaks springs from our experience with Christ in desperate and painful situations such as wilderness experiences, prison cells, on crosses, and in the lives of those who have put Christ as the Lord and center of their lives.

One of the useful insights into the development of humility is the distinction the world makes between the "haves" and the "have-nots," being "nothing" and being "something," being "somebody" versus "nobody." Paul notes the distinction in

Galatians 6:3; *"If anyone thinks they are something when they are not, they deceive themselves."*

This distinction is a theme which weaves its way through Philippians as Paul describes his journey with Christ as **downward** in contrast to the **upward** perspective of the world—from the "somethingness" of education, position, authority, control, and the influence of his previous life, to the "nothingness" attained by following Christ. Our success in imitating Christ depends on how deep our identity-perspective is rooted in him—in who he is, what he stands for, and who we are to be as a result.

Humility is never a denial of our worth or value innately but a transplanting of our identity on new soil. We were created by God for a purpose. As Christians our new identity is now rooted in Christ. Paul said; *"Therefore, if anyone is in Christ he is a new creation, the old has gone, the new has come."* (2 CORINTHIANS 5:17) It is no longer necessary to conform to a worldly definition of who we should be. Notice Jesus' temptation experience in the wilderness as an example.

Then Jesus was led by the Spirit into the wilderness to be tempted by the devil. After fasting forty days and forty nights, he was hungry. The tempter came to him and said, "If you are the Son of God, tell these stones to become bread." Jesus answered, "It is written: 'Man shall not live on bread alone, but on every word that comes from the mouth of God'" Then the devil took him to the holy city and had him stand on the highest point of the temple. "If you are the Son of God," he said, "throw yourself down. For it is written: "'He will command his angels concerning you, and they will lift you up in their hands, so that you will not strike your foot against a stone.'" Jesus answered him, "It is also written: 'Do not put the Lord your God to the test.' " Again, the devil took him to a very high mountain and showed him all the kingdoms of the world and their splendor. "All this I will give you," he said, "if you will bow down and worship me." Jesus said to him, "Away from me, Satan! For it is written: 'Worship the Lord your God, and serve him only.' "(MATTHEW 4:1-10; LUKE 4:1-13)

Satan was attacking Jesus' confidence in his identity-perspective when he said, *"If you are the Son of God . . ."* Why an "if" unless Jesus' identity-perspective was vulnerable? Satan was probing for self-doubt in Jesus' view of himself by showing him all the kingdoms of the world and their splendor as the rightful entitlement of the Son of God and true confirmation of his identity; and not just one kingdom but all of them.

If Jesus fell to the temptation to confirm his identity from ruling earthly kingdoms, one or a few would never be enough as long as there were others to be ruled. Once we cross over to the dark side it's all or nothing. If a person, for example, builds her confidence and identity by growing her assets she will always live under the depressing shadow of those who have more. And there will always be those who have more.

Why was Jesus even tempted, having already experienced heaven and the presence of God? What would the world's kingdoms have to offer in comparison to being in the presence of God? Remember, these temptations came after forty days of fasting when Jesus felt the full weight of his humanity. Suffering, hunger, loss, or sense of entitlement can jade one's cognitive processes to a point when the kingdoms of the world appear to have a lot to offer. No more poverty, hunger or thirst, bearing the ridicule of being a lowly carpenter, being disrespected as an ignorant and uneducated peasant. Jesus could have been the best, greatest, richest, and most of all, the most respected man in the world—the ultimate icon of worldly success. Yet, his true identity and the road to nothingness led him a different way. And for us, it's the only way.

Chapter Two

OUR NOTHINGNESS
BEFORE GOD

*But our citizenship is in heaven. And we eagerly await a Savior
from there, the Lord Jesus Christ, who, by the power that enables
him to bring everything under his control, will transform
our lowly bodies so that they will be like his glorious body.*
(PHILIPPIANS 3:20-21)

In the above passage Paul makes the contrast between
Christ's *glorious body* and our *lowly body*. Only through the
power of God do we have any hope of a glorious body. As
we will see, the understanding of our nothingness before God—
the difference between our humanity and God's nature, and our
complete dependence on him—is paramount to our accepting the
call to a life of humility.

In order to have a better idea of what Paul means when he
says, Jesus emptied himself and became nothing, it is important
to recall how Paul defines the idea in PHILIPPIANS 2.

*Who, being in very nature God, did not consider equality with
God something to be grasped; rather, he made himself nothing
by taking the very **nature of a servant**, being made in **human
likeness**. And being found in **appearance as a man**, he*

humbled himself by ***becoming obedient*** *to death—even death on a cross!* [emphasis mine]

I emphasized several words to show the main characteristics necessary for Jesus to become nothing. Service, humility, and obedience are all a part of his complete self-denial. But notice how the humanity of Christ, his *being made in human likeness and being found in appearance as a man*, is also a significant part of that nothingness.

To God humanity is "nothing," which shows the huge chasm between our nature and God's. It's not a "nothing" defined by non-existence, purposelessness, or worthlessness, but a "nothing" defined by comparison—between the finite and the infinite, and the created and the ultimate.

Jesus was not considered "nothing" or "empty" until he took on human likeness, but his willingness to serve and put others' needs before his own, his humility, and obedience were critical to his willingness to take human form. Jesus might have begun his human journey at the incarnation but all of these other spiritual virtues had to be firmly in place at the beginning and end of his earthly journey. The imitation of Christ's nothingness means the virtues of serving, humility, and obedience must be continually incorporated into our lives.

By the time Jesus died on the cross, he had literally given his all. He emptied himself to become nothing. Like when you take a full pitcher of water and pour it all out, Jesus poured himself out completely. There was nothing left to give. He died having completed the task of going through an excruciating death without sinning. He committed his spirit to God with no bitterness, anger, hate, or sense of entitlement in his heart—just humility, complete self-denial, and obedience. These are the footsteps we have been commanded to follow.

As mentioned above, "nothing" is a statement of contrast, between our flesh and God's deity. We are nothing but finite specks of dust in a massive universe sustained completely by the power of God. Because of modern telescopes, we have tremendous possibilities than in past times to look far into space for a better understanding of the complexities of the universe. Complexities so beyond our ability to duplicate that the contemplation of the universe's marvels has the potential of bringing us to a deeper level of humility. How that works will be explained later.

Therefore, modern man has a greater opportunity to investigate our universe and to respond accordingly. The only way we can persevere on a journey to complete self-denial is if we recognize our physical and spiritual nothingness in comparison to God's eternal nature.

The Holiness of God

In order to understand more fully our "nothingness" before God, I'm introducing some ideas associated with God's holiness that I hope will be helpful.

The "holiness" of God is a theme that runs throughout the entire Bible. God commands his people to be holy as he is holy. (Leviticus 11:44) "Separation" is the basic idea of holiness and was used initially most often in reference to certain days, sacred objects, and, of course, the Holy of Holies in the early Tabernacle to its final resting place in the temple in Jerusalem.

Those places, days, and objects were considered "separate" from all others and were expected to be treated and handled as such. God also regarded Israel as a Holy Nation and warned the Israelites to hold their allegiance to him. Isaiah said, *"Come out from them and be separate, says the Lord. Touch no unclean thing, and I will receive you."* (ISAIAH 52:11)

Normally, when we consider the idea of holiness, we attempt to apply the biblical admonishments to be holy to our behavior. Yet, the origin of the biblical idea of holiness is not rooted in behavior, though this has important application to Christian living.

It is understandable how the idea of "holy" has come to mean an emphasis on how we should live and act. Yet, that is not how we should understand the idea as it relates to God. The first instance when the idea of holiness is applied to God was when Moses approached the "burning bush" and God said to him; *"Take off your sandals, for the place where you are standing is holy ground." Then he said, "I am the God of your father, the God of Abraham, the God of Isaac and the God of Jacob." At this, Moses hid his face, because he was afraid to look at God."* (EXODUS 3:5-6)

God is holy and separate from us because of his nature, entirely unlike humankind and completely "other" than anything we are or have ever experienced. The ground was not holy because of any actions on God's part, but because of God's nature and presence—his "otherness" in regards to his essential being.

What we see in Moses' reaction to the holiness of God is both an amazement and allurement to the mysteriousness and unexplainable, but also a strong aversion to the presence of God. There is both a drawing and repelling effect to the mysteriousness involved with the nature of God—something that draws us in, but also brings us to our knees.

Rudolf Otto, a Jewish-German Theologian in the middle of the 20th century, authored the classic work, *The Idea of the Holy*. In it he traces the meaning of "holy" from its Hebrew and Semitic roots to its meaning in Greek and Latin translations. He stresses that in its original form the Hebrew word for "holy" had an emphasis on the mysterious and unexplainable.

Obviously, the call to be holy as God is holy involves the radical lifestyle we are expected to live—what we do. But being holy more fundamentally involves who we are, and most importantly who we envision ourselves to be. To fully and effectively serve a holy God with a grateful willing heart, a transformation in our identity-perspective must first take place.

Rudolf Otto discussed the impact of being in the mere presence of God, in particular, how it arouses the inherent realization of our dependence on a being with more power and intelligence. For example, when pleading in the presence of God for the lives of the men of Sodom, Abraham said, *"Now that I have been so bold as to speak to the Lord, though I am nothing but dust and ashes, . . ."* (GENESIS 18:27) In regards to this situation, Otto stated:

> *There you have a self-confessed "feeling of dependence," which is yet at the same time more than, and something other than, rather than, merely a feeling of dependence. Desiring to give it a name of its own, I propose to call it "creature-consciousness" or creature feeling. It is the emotion of a creature, abased and overwhelmed by its own nothingness in contrast to that which is supreme above all creatures.*

"Creature-consciousness" is the foundational state of mind on. which humility is built. Simply put, it is when we fully recognize we are the creatures and God is the creator. Creature-consciousness is ignited only when we objectively perceive ourselves in comparison to the Almighty.

In a world governed by physical law, how do we deepen our awareness of the presence of God? Where can we find our own "burning bush" experiences that inspire our "creature-consciousness?"

We might never experience a miraculous burning bush, but the burning bushes are still there, we just need to see them. Though Christianity is rooted in historical fact, God never intended for the study and understanding of history to be the only means through which a "sense" of the miraculous can be experienced. Looking for God in the past is important, but God is also powerfully at work in the present.

The miracle of the burning bush was that it was burning but not consumed by the flames. The sun has been burning since the creation of the universe and is still unconsumed. And we stand in its presence every day and marvel at the beauty of sunrises and sunsets.

Part of our problem with being able to stand in awe of the creation involves the physical laws that control the world in which we live. The predictability and consistency of these laws lull us into a state of mind unimpressed by the normalcy of the world around us. We were born into a world where the sun rises and sets like clockwork and when something becomes "normal," for whatever reasons, it no longer has an inspiring impact on us.

When the Israelites ran out of food after Moses led them from Egypt into the desert, God miraculously gave them manna to eat. At first, the people were inspired and thankful for the miracle. When the manna became a normal part of life and was expected every day, the inspiration and gratitude faded into disgruntlement. The "manna" no longer had the miraculous aura about it.

To stand in awe of what we see, reality must be viewed as the "miraculous" work of God—an ongoing result of the infinite power of God. We define a miracle as the "unexplainable" in a cause-and-effect explainable world—an event outside a world governed by physical law. But what is the source of those laws? Why is there such intricate and complex design to our existence and not complete chaos?

To God the "unexplainable" is a term unique to the finite mind and nothing more than God's manipulation of physical law to confirm his message and accomplish his purposes. The reality of laws implies intelligence behind those laws. The existence of God is the only option to explain what is to us unexplainable.

The existence of our world forces us to either turn a deaf ear to any discussion of the evidence for the supernatural, or to look for answers from the spiritual realm. The sensible explanation for our experience in the world around us involves the existence of two realms—the natural and the supernatural.

Faith is the key which unlocks the inspiring effect of the supernatural, but only a correctly defined faith. The writer to the Hebrews defines faith in the following way: *"Now faith is confidence in what we hope for and assurance about what we **do not see**."* (HEBREWS 11:1) [Emphasis mine] After seeing the wounds on Jesus' resurrected body and believing, Thomas was told the following by Jesus; *"Because you have seen me, you have believed; **blessed are those who have not seen** and yet have believed."* (JOHN 20:28) [Emphasis mine]

In other words, there is an experience beyond where the observation of miracles alone can take us, an experience which Jesus sets forth as the most blessed. That is, coming to faith and humility by observing and internalizing everything we see as a miracle so to speak. All of existence is in essence a burning bush — unsustainable without supernatural power. "Seeing through" the physical world and embracing the reality of the existence of God is what a faith experience is all about and where the journey to the humility of Christ begins.

An example of this experience is found in 2 Kings 6:8-17 concerning the prophet Elisha. The King of Aram was at war with the King of Israel. Elisha advised the King of Israel regarding the enemy's offensive plans which continued to frustrate the King of Aram, who suspected a spy among his commanders. Informed that Elisha was the problem, part of the Aramean army was dispatched to the town of Dothan where Elisha lived and surrounded it with the intention of capturing him.

When the servant of Elisha awoke the following day and saw the Arameans encircling the town, he was naturally afraid and looked to Elisha for a solution. Elisha reassured him that those protecting them were far more numerous than those of the Aramean forces, and prayed, *"Open his eyes, Lord, so that he may see."* And the narrative goes on to state; . . . *"then the Lord opened the servant's eyes, and he looked and saw the hills full of horses and chariots of fire all around Elisha."*

The lesson to this story involves the contrasting emotional reactions of Elisha and his servant to the presence of the Aramean army. Unable to "see through" or beyond the physical presence of the enemy, the servant was left with his fear. Elisha was fearless because he was a man of faith centered on the reality of things "unseen." Unless we grow in our conviction that a holy God actually exists, completely different from us with powers beyond our comprehension, the physical armies of the enemy will always leave us fearful and block us from seeing by faith the eternal forces of God.

Being overwhelmed by our own nothingness, as Rudolf Otto puts it, is only accomplished when we stand in the presence of God. Though we do not physically see him, we see him through the eyes of faith, and that encounter must become as personal as a "personal" face to face encounter. What we see through the eyes of faith depends on the quality of our meditation, study, and prayer. It is through these avenues that our eyes of faith develop their full "see-through" potential.

As our faith deepens our convictions in turn become centered on the reality that as disciples of Christ we are always in the presence of God. That is part of our identity as his children. That faith-experience is what empowers us to keep our identity-perspective rooted in Christ. It is only through faith that we have the chance to stay overwhelmed by our own nothingness, yet confident as we stand in the presence of God.

The writer of the book of Hebrews stated: *"Therefore, brothers and sisters, since we have confidence to enter the Most Holy Place by the blood of Jesus, by a new and living way opened for us through the curtain, that is, his body, and since we have a great priest over the house of God, let us draw near to God with a sincere heart and with the full assurance that faith brings, having our hearts sprinkled to cleanse us from a guilty conscience and having our bodies washed with pure water."* (HEBREWS 10:19-21) [Emphasis mine]

To sum up this section, our fear of God and amazement at the reality of the miraculous shows the stark contrast between our power and God's. Our world and his. Otherwise, we wouldn't be so amazed, fearful, and in such awe. Understanding his holiness is the key to our creature-consciousness and the rationale for our humility.

We should be thankful that God put us in an environment in which we can be amazed by not only the miraculous working of God throughout history, but also by the wonder and beauty of nature all around us—an environment in which we can know that there is an intelligent power beyond our own—a massive "burning bush" capable of bringing us to a "creature-consciousness" in the presence of a holy God.

Becoming "Nothing": An Intelligent Endeavor

Many avoid religion because they consider it driven mainly by weak-minded emotionalism, void of any logical rationale. Christianity is thought to be anti-intellectual because of the assumption that Christ's teaching on humility and self-denial implies that we are to follow him blindly—that the use of our intellect and proper reasoning must be denied. However, our intellect is God-given and necessary to evaluate the evidence for the existence of God and to be convinced that a life of humility is the only way to have a relationship with him.

God expects us to use our intellect and reasoning to cut through our subjective biases to correctly process the evidence for his existence so that our humility and self-denial have a rationale, and not just a result of depression, poor self-image, or feelings of guilt. No one can withstand the intensity of the journey into the nothingness of Christ without being absolutely convinced that it leads to God. And the correct use of our intellectual abilities is critical to the development of that conviction.

There is no place in the biblical record that allows us on Judgment Day to plea that we did not know how to live because the evidence was too confusing. "Not knowing" or "not understanding" are not options, so maintaining a keen use of the intellect is critical to knowing God.

God intends for our intellect to bring us to the recognition of our desperate need for him and not to produce arrogance and a stand-off, so to speak, between our intellect and his. The desperation which results from our deepest needs not being met stimulates our full intellectual potential to view the evidence for God more objectively. Desperation implies our inability to meet our own needs and frees the mind and heart of pride and arrogance—sins which neutralize the penetrating effect of God's evidence in our hearts.

Notice the example of Abraham. He was told to sacrifice his son, Isaac, as proof of his devotion to God (Genesis 22). Abraham's willingness to obey brought him to a state of "nothingness" and "emptiness" before God, which enabled him to put aside his pride and belief in his own capabilities and to realistically ponder his dilemma. He was out of options and powerless. His only choice was to believe in something he had never seen or heard of—God's power to raise from the dead the child he was about to kill. The writer of Hebrews puts it this way: *"Abraham reasoned that God could even raise the dead."* (Hebrews 11:19) Abraham's situation shows that proper reasoning and use of the intellect is ignited in seemingly hopeless situations when our eyes are opened to the limits of our humanity and our need for a higher power.

Furthermore, if we pride ourselves on our intellectual abilities and cannot find solutions for the most important issues in life, then we must ask ourselves just how intelligent are we? The desperation we need to change our lives comes from the realization of how dependent on God we are, and how meaningless life is without him. Without his power we have no hope, no hope at all.

Humility allows us to process evidence objectively and to reach accurate conclusions. For example, most have been taught that the understanding of the Bible is a matter of personal interpretation. Yet, to reach a correct objective interpretation personal biases and traditions must be denied, and the question must be raised consistently, what does the Bible actually say? Not, what do I want it to say? As long as we approach the Bible with pride in our traditions, family religious history, our own need to be right, and concern over what others think, we will never be able to live by what is true.

The world is on cruise control, not asking the pertinent questions involving our origin, purpose, and destiny. Humankind's success in mathematics, science, and technology has led to an illusion that the answers to life can be found without the need for a God. This move away from God is a relatively modern social movement compared to the rest of history when people without modern advancements in medicine and technology were more aware of the desperation of their circumstances. When in desperate situations we all have a tendency to look beyond ourselves and upward which is why religion was at the center of ancient and pre-modern civilizations.

As we excel in our attainment of knowledge useful to the preservation and quality of life we tend to push the need for God further and further away. What we often refer to as God becomes what Dietrich Bonhoeffer, the famous German theologian, called, "The God of the Boundaries." We tend to keep God away from those areas of life we believe we can control. When we get sick we simply go to the doctor, whereas, pre-modern people would pray.

God is someone we keep on the borders which surround our abilities. Once we recognize that we are beyond our abilities we inherently turn to God personally or we had least raise the question regarding the possibility of his existence. Bonhoeffer's challenge is to invite God from the borders of our lives into the center of the camp.

Identity-Perspective and Spiritual Blindness

In Acts chapters 9 and 22 we have a record of Paul's conversion to Christ. Since we introduced Paul's life as part of our discussion in chapter one it will do us well to mention his conversion. While Paul was leading a group of Pharisees to the town of Damascus to persecute Jews who had become Christians, Jesus appeared to him and blinded him.

Why did Jesus choose to blind him? Why not just encourage Paul to rethink his position, or challenge him on his incorrect interpretation of the messianic passages in the Old Testament? The blindness appears to have had the intention to show that the issues were not only the limitations of Paul's knowledge, but to also to demonstrate how spiritually blind he was. Though extremely knowledgeable concerning the contents of the Old Testament, Paul needed to understand the absolute futility of his thinking process and how it was leading him away from the Christ rather than to him. What he needed was humility which would in turn open his eyes to his "nothingness" before God.

Paul was blinded physically to put him into a helpless situation where God could "reboot" a way of thinking which was leading Paul to the murder of innocent disciples of Christ in Damascus. From God's point of view, even with all of his education, recognition, and aspiring future, Paul could not have been further from the truth—utterly and completely blind spiritually. His physical blindness opened the door to the desperation he needed to deal with his pride over success and position and to hear the voice of God.

Another example of spiritual blindness is recorded in JOHN 9 and provides us further insight into the power of nothingness. In this situation, Jesus restored the sight of a man born blind. Notice the context of the miracle:

> As he went along, he saw a man blind from birth. His disciples asked him, "Rabbi, who sinned, this man or his parents, that he was born blind?" "Neither this man nor his parents sinned," said Jesus, "but this happened so that the works of God might be displayed in him. As long as it is day, we must do the works of him who sent me. Night is coming, when no one can work. While I am in the world, I am the light of the world." After saying this, he spit on the ground, made some mud with the saliva, and put it on the man's eyes. "Go," he told him, "wash in the Pool of Siloam" (this word means "Sent"). So the man went and washed, and came home seeing. (JOHN 9: 1-7)

In the first century Jewish theology often maintained disease or disability to be a result of sin and God's discipline. A man born blind posed an interesting question—if blindness was a result of sin and a man is born with such a severe disability, how can he be held accountable? Was he born with the sin of his parents?

Jesus clarifies that the origin of the blindness was not sin but an opportunity for the glory of God to be demonstrated. Here is a situation when desperation and the glory of God are both evident. This man was obviously at the low end of the social scale and had lived under the label of being "cursed by God" all of his life. So, what else did God have in mind for this man? Beyond the actual healing, were there other works to which Jesus referred? He did use the plural, "works."

Because healing was considered a "work" in the tradition of the Pharisees, it was forbidden on the Sabbath. Therefore, the Pharisees doubted the credibility of the miracle. After they initially questioned the man and his parents, they again called in the man who had been healed to question him. When challenged by the former blind man as to why they were unable to grasp the reality of the situation—that he had indeed been healed—the Pharisees hurled insults at him and threw him out.

John records Jesus' response to the man's rejection by the Pharisees:

> Jesus heard that they had thrown him out, and when he found him, he said, "Do you believe in the Son of Man?" "Who is he, sir?" the man asked. "Tell me so that I may believe in him." Jesus said, "You have now seen him; in fact, he is the one speaking with you." Then the man said, "Lord, I believe," and he worshiped him. Jesus said, "For judgment I have come into this world, so that the blind will see and those who see will become blind." Some Pharisees who were with him heard him say this and asked, "What? Are we blind too?" Jesus said, "If you were blind, you would not be guilty of sin; but now that you claim you can see, your guilt remains. (vss. 35-41)

The main lesson of this healing was not only to show the power and compassion of God, but also to demonstrate how the position of "nothing" has powerful implications for our character and our witness for Christ. Remember, this man stood in the meeting place of the Pharisees, boldly and confidently proclaiming the reality of the miracle which the Pharisees disputed. He was confident because his identity-perspective was not polluted with concerns over how people viewed him or whether he might jeopardize his social standing and chances for a successful financial future. He knew he was a "nobody." And herein lies the power of nothingness.

Notice the interchange between the Pharisees and the healed man:

> A second time they summoned the man who had been blind. "Give glory to God by telling the truth," they said. "We know this man is a sinner." He replied, "Whether he is a sinner or not, I don't know. One thing I do know. I was blind but now I see!" Then they asked him, "What did he do to you? How did he open your eyes?" He answered, "I have told you already and you did not listen. Why do you want to hear it again? Do you want to become his disciples too?" Then they hurled insults at him and said, "You are this fellow's disciple! We are disciples of Moses! We know that God spoke to Moses, but as for this fellow, we don't even know where he comes from." The man answered, "Now that is remarkable! You don't know where he comes from, yet he opened my eyes. We know that God does not listen to sinners. He listens to the godly person who does his will. Nobody has ever heard of opening the eyes of a man born blind. If this man were not from God, he could do nothing." To this they replied, "You were steeped in sin at birth; how dare you lecture us!" And they threw him out. (vss 24-34)

The Pharisees intimidated the people by their knowledge and the prestigious positions they occupied, and therefore, this man was shunned and ridiculed his whole life. With their legalistic judgments, the Pharisees were nothing more than spiritual bullies, but because this man's identity-perspective was intact he would have nothing to do with it. He had no worries about further ridicule. He had grown up with it. He had no concerns about disappointing his family. He had been a disappointment his whole life. He had no fear of being cast out of the synagogue. He was never welcome in the first place. Threaten him with death? He had probably already prayed that he would die.

How much more abuse could you possibly put on a man who already realizes he is nothing? What could you possibly take from him that would produce such a fear of loss to cause him to compromise the truth? It often gets to the point in life when truth is all we really have. The healed blind man had the truth— he was able to see—and no one had the power to take that truth from him. That's the power of an identity-perspective rooted in the realities of nothingness and objective truth.

This is a man at the low end of society—unclean, outcast, and cursed—up against the top tier of society, and yet he never even flinches. The Pharisees' minds were cluttered because of their unrestrained need for position and title. If they were to admit to the clear evidence standing before them, they would have to admit that Jesus really was the Messiah and that would mean the end to any future in Judaism.

On the other hand, because of the healed man's circumstances, his need for the respect of others through position and title had never been ignited or developed so there was no need to compromise the truth. He had absolutely nothing to lose, because there was nothing he had acquired. Through his "nothingness," though blind, he was able to see much more than the physical world around him.

The healed man had obviously been brought to his state of nothingness through very difficult circumstances. Not many of us are as privileged. We have to face the same challenge as the

Pharisees—to overcome an inflated view of ourselves and a distorted identity-perspective through which we judge others. Unfortunately, Pharisaism occupies a large part of all of our hearts. But with humility it can be overcome.

Chapter Three

OUR "SUCCESS" AND THE HUMILITY OF CHRIST

If someone else thinks they have reasons to put confidence in the flesh, I have more: circumcised on the eighth day, of the people of Israel, of the tribe of Benjamin, a Hebrew of Hebrews; in regard to the law, a Pharisee; as for zeal, persecuting the church; as for righteousness based on the law, faultless. (PHILIPPIANS 3:4-6)

In the passage quoted above, Paul gives us his pre-Christian resume — quite impressive for a first century Jew to say the least. In his previous world Paul was an extraordinarily accomplished and successful man, having rooted his identity and sense of well-being in education, position, and legalistic exactness. Though there is some relationship between being and doing, it is important to note here is that most of Paul's resume emphasized who he was and not so much on what he did. Paul was engrossed with his image and who he viewed himself to have become. He had a bad case of "position addiction."

For Paul, education and scholastic mentoring were not just quests for knowledge about God but also quests for title, position, influence, and most of all, to be the "best." Commenting on his past life in Judaism, Paul stated, *"I was advancing in Judaism beyond many of my own age among my people and was extremely zealous for the traditions of my fathers."* (GALATIANS 1:14)

Yet, after he became a disciple of Christ he considered all of these accomplishments and titles as nothing more than garbage and dung.

> *But whatever were gains to me I now consider loss for the sake of Christ. What is more, I consider everything a loss because of the surpassing worth of knowing Christ Jesus my Lord, for whose sake I have lost all things. I consider them garbage, that I may gain Christ and be found in him, not having a righteousness of my own that comes from the law, but that which is through faith in Christ—the righteousness that comes from God on the basis of faith.* (PHILIPPIANS 3:7-9)

The word "garbage" can also be translated, "dung," or, "manure," if we keep in mind that without modern paper, plastic, or glass goods to discard nor modern sewer systems in place, ancient rubbish consisted largely of human and animal waste. That was the image in Paul's mind.

In the phrase where Paul says, *"But whatever were gains to me I now consider loss for the sake of Christ,"* the word, "now," is important here to note. It indicates a process of growth in spiritual perspective and realization—from when the "gains" were considered of value to when they were considered a "loss."

The "gains" Paul mentions were a deep part of his upbringing — pride, identity, and sense of security. Paul wasn't just a Hebrew. In his mind, he was a "Hebrew of Hebrews"—a cut above everybody else—with a future destined for greatness. In order to follow Christ he had to undergo intense challenges to get to the point that these accomplishments were considered valueless, belonging only in the dung heap.

In his delusional state, Paul viewed himself as perfect in obedience to the old laws and the legalistic traditions that followed—he considered himself "faultless." Not only was this a perspective perverted by personal arrogance but also one of spiritual blindness—an indication of how our drive for success can lead to delusion. Notice the contrast in the contents of the following Scripture:

The Lord looks down from heaven on all mankind to see if there are any who understand, any who seek God. All have turned away, all have become corrupt; there is no one who does good, not even one. (PSALM 14:2-3)

Obviously, God's view of Paul was opposite to Paul's view of himself. Closing the gap between these two perspectives in our own lives is the central theme of this book. It involves not only a transition in behavior but more so a transition in mindset. Paul's letter to the Philippians offers great insight into Paul's transition from his self-delusion of greatness to the realization of his true identity before God.

We need to pursue the question regarding why Paul termed his previous success with such intense imagery depicting one of the most disgusting parts of human existence—human waste, as discussed above. Why throw all of these accomplishments to the dung heap? Why such a tension between success and knowing Christ? Aren't we to assume that success is a blessing from God?

Certainly, God used Paul's scholastic Jewish upbringing to defend Christianity against the legalism of Judaism and the philosophies of the Greek world. Paul's classic letter to the Romans in the New Testament is an example of his keen understanding of the first century issues regarding the separation of Christianity and Judaism, and the universal application of that separation.

In the 16th century from a small lecture hall at the Castle Church in Wittenberg, Germany, with his teachings on the Paul's letter to the Romans, Martin Luther ignited the Protestant Reformation Movement against the traditions of the Catholic Church. The contents of the book of Romans historically, as well as its present relevancy, show that God's use of Paul's intellectual "success" continues to impact disciples around the world. However, objectively speaking Paul was just a vessel through whom God was working.

So, it is not Paul's scholastic accomplishments or influence that was the problem, but rather, his unhealthy dependence on knowledge and influence as a foundational part of his self-esteem and identity-perspective. It's obvious from Psalm 14 quoted above that God's view of Humankind is radically different from Paul's pre-Christian perspective about himself.

Yet, how could someone so accomplished and recognized in his knowledge of the Scriptures and passionate in his zeal to protect the integrity of the Jewish faith, be so wrong? Paul seemed very sincere about what he believed. Yet, sincerity only involves the quality of our motivation and never the confirmation of truth.

The problem with Paul like the rest of humankind was pride. Pride is a "blinder"—a protective emotional wall which shields us from the pain of seeing all our reality and taking responsibility for our mistakes before others and God. Prideful people certainly experience some level of sorrow in their lives, but never at a deep enough level to bring about genuine and lasting change. Notice how Paul contrasts two different responses to our realization of sin:

Godly sorrow brings repentance that leads to salvation and leaves no regret, but worldly sorrow brings death. See what this godly sorrow has produced in you: what earnestness, what eagerness to clear yourselves, what indignation, what alarm, what longing, what concern, what readiness to see justice done. (2 CORINTHIANS 7:10-11)

Obvious from this passage is the incredible power godly sorrow can have in our lives. It melts away all pretensions of self-righteousness and tenderizes the heart which results in genuineness, purity of motives, and a deep concern to do the right thing. Repentance was never meant to be a "biting the bullet" agonizing type of experience, but an opportunity to be transformed into an honest, genuine, and courageous person. In one of Peter's sermons, he stated, *"Repent, then, and turn to God, so that your sins may be wiped out, that times of refreshing may come from the Lord . . ."* (ACTS 3:19).

In elaboration of the importance of courage when facing truth, it should be said that godly sorrow not only produces a greater courage to face the truth as we grow in our concern and earnestness to confront our sin, but courage must also precede godly sorrow to some extent. Godly sorrow is a result of opening the eyes of our hearts and taking a deep honest look into God's truth about who we really are; and that takes courage. The hardest part of Christianity is the daily and consistent decision to walk in the light.

Our only other option is a superficial disingenuous worldly sorrow that brings death. People with this level of sorrow feel only enough sorrow to ease the most agonizing of guilt pains. They might do some "good" deeds to ease their consciences, but soon return to a state of denying, ignoring, or intellectualizing away the truth. That, however, only leads to a hardening of the heart and to consciences that . . . *have been seared as with a hot iron,* as Paul describes in 1 TIMOTHY 4:2, and ultimately to spiritual death.

God's Nature and Our "Success"

By the time we meet Jesus in life, we are entrapped by a sinful nature determined to fulfill the many pleasures of the self. James puts it this way: *"What causes fights and quarrels among you? Don't they come from your desires that battle within you? You desire but do not have, so you kill. You covet but you cannot get what you want, so you quarrel and fight. You do not have because you do not ask God. When you ask, you do not receive, because you ask with wrong motives, that you may spend what you get on your pleasures."* (JAMES 4:1-3)

Prominence and recognition are some of the most sought after pleasures in life. Not a prominence and recognition as in the case of Joseph in the Old Testament, raised up by God because of his integrity and devotion to God, but a self-centered desire for success and the consequent recognition.

An unhealthy need for success and respect pollutes and undermines any attempt at living a selfless Christian life. Life becomes all about us. Our "Christian" example ends up only a projection of religion, a powerless shielded religiosity rooted in our insecurity of others coming to a knowledge of the real truths in our lives—the real failures.

Many hide behind the walls of education, title, accomplishment, and wealth, hopefully to keep others from wondering about the spiritual integrity of their lives. With the need to be **someone** who has achieved **something** so entrenched in our sinful natures, it is only with the power of God are we able to move from a world which drives us to be something, to an unseen world which allows us to be nothing and content at the same time.

We define success as a result of certain standards of behavior. Whatever our goals, there are actions necessary to keep from being a failure and which insure success. God is not successful in that sense. He has no obstacles to overcome or behavior to enact in order to be successful. He is by **nature** successful. It is impossible for him to be unsuccessful.

If we believe God is perfection, then he has nothing to achieve. God just is. He is successful just being God. Was God a "nobody" and the creation of the world made him a "somebody"? Did he move from the "have-nots" to the "haves" now that he owns the universe and everything in it? He certainly completed the task. But how can God be successful as we define success when there is no chance of failure? It's almost an insult to God to use the word success or to say, "Hey God, great job!" "Great" and "God" are redundant terms, completely synonymous.

In Mark 9 a man brings his son to Jesus to be healed. After he describes his son's condition, the man said, *"But if you can do anything, take pity on us and help us." "If you can?" said Jesus. "Everything is possible for one who believes"* (MARK 9:22-23) In other words, there are no "ifs" with God, nor levels of greatness, just ultimate being.

A God who is love certainly celebrates with the success and progress of his children, but that in no way implies he is impressed by that success. As far as God is concerned everything comes from him anyway. It's impossible to impress an intelligence with the power to create the universe out of nothing or guide the outcome of human history. What has humankind ever achieved that would qualify in the league in which God operates?

Scientific and technological advances have certainly led to the improvement of the quality of life, but have in no way provided a solution to the real problems in our world—the most important being the reality of death. Even though there is much promise in our ability to extend life by the use of modern medicine, death is still at the end of it all. And death always raises the question of God's existence.

Whether we live 500 or 1000 years longer what difference does it make in the eternal scheme of things? How does one compare 1000 years with eternity? And if there is no eternity as some claim, then why extend life at all? Why not get death over with?

Along with having no answers to physical death, spiritual death is all the more problematic. Paul described it this way when he wrote to the Ephesians:

> As for you, you were dead in your transgressions and sins, in which you used to live when you followed the ways of this world and of the ruler of the kingdom of the air, the spirit who is now at work in those who are disobedient. All of us also lived among them at one time, gratifying the cravings of our flesh and following its desires and thoughts. Like the rest, we were by nature deserving of wrath. (EPHESIANS 2:1-5)

Even though the Ephesians were still alive physically when Paul wrote to them, he describes their former life outside of Christ as being "dead." People mistakenly confuse the energy put forth by . . . *gratifying the cravings of our flesh and following its desires and thoughts* . . . as life, when in reality without God it is a symptom of spiritual death.

This inescapable dilemma of death, both physically and spiritually, makes the resurrection of Christ all the more appealing, necessary, and from a theological perspective, logical. A future resurrection is a necessary and key component of any legitimate theological or philosophical framework.

Is it a coincidence that a carpenter's son just happened to come up with the need for resurrection, preached that he was the resurrection and the life, and then demonstrated by his own resurrection that he truly represented the ultimate power of God? No other human being has ever demonstrated that level of power. Jesus provides the only reasonable and verifiable solution to life's main dilemmas. Therefore, his teachings are the only true measure of success.

Our Fear of the Feelings of Guilt

This is the verdict: Light has come into the world, but people loved darkness instead of light because their deeds were evil. Everyone who does evil hates the light, and will not come into the light for fear that their deeds will be exposed. (JOHN 3:19-20)

The reason for the death of Christ is that we are all guilty of sin. No one is exempt. That is the objective truth regardless of how we feel. Unfortunately, the feelings of guilt are some of the most dreaded feelings in life. We avoid feeling guilty and bad about things that we do through denial and self-justification. People hate coming into the light, and often hide behind success and personal achievement.

Some psychologists caution their clients' about involvement in religion and, in particular, exposure to preaching because of the possibility of being left with the feelings of guilt. This is understandable in a world which for the most part no longer believes in objective truth. And we must admit that guilt has no rationale in a world guided by subjective relativism—the idea that all morals, values, and the meaning of reality itself, are relative and left to individual interpretation. But in God's world relativism and subjectivism do not exist. There is an ultimate right and wrong. And when we do wrong we are guilty.

Feelings of guilt are a powerful force and avoiding them is a major concern in all of our lives. There have been numerous incidences when someone would commit a crime and years later turn themselves in because the guilty feelings were so intense. To avoid the feelings of guilt we must either change what is wrong-thinking and behavior, or guilt will lead us to self-justification, the suppression of feelings, self-medication through alcohol and drugs, and hardening of the heart and conscience.

Just as Adam tried to hide his guilt from God in the Garden of Eden, we hide much the same way through denial and self-justification. God intends our consciences to guide us in our decisions. When our consciences lose their sensitivity because of repeated sins and continual self-justification, we are left with only raw erratic self-serving emotions to guide our way.

For example, the reason for most arguments in relationships involves people not taking responsibility for their sins, and blaming their sins on the actions of others, and blaming God. Adam blamed Eve for his sin and we often blame circumstances and others for ours. Trying to avoid the feelings of guilt by not taking responsibility for our sins can lead us to some pretty dark and scary places. The infamous mass-murderer, Charles Manson, attempted to defend himself at his trial by arguing that the state was more responsible for his actions than he personally was because society molded him and was, therefore, the real criminal.

Inappropriate Guilt

In our discussion of guilt, it is important to point out that there is also such a thing as "inappropriate" guilt — guilt that people should **not** feel. For example, people who have been abused physically, emotionally, or sexually are often left with inappropriate feelings of guilt because their abusers have convinced them that they are the problem.

Regarding faith and guilt, even though a particular faith tradition does not reflect the will of God as the traditions of the Pharisees, violating it can leave one with deep guilty feelings because of an uneducated conscience. Another example of inappropriate guilt involves our struggle to accept God's forgiveness. This is the case when the light of God's truth does not penetrate the emotions to relieve the feelings of condemnation, even after we become Christians.

God created us with emotions such as feelings of guilt to guide our reactions and consequent behavior. Reason impacts and validates our emotions but emotions are the driving forces in our lives. Even an outburst of anger must first go through some sort of reasoning and justifying process prior to the outburst itself. Though many of our thoughts and actions do not objectively "make sense," we always seem to have a way to make sense of our shortcomings through self-justification and delusion.

Spiritual conviction is the correct emotional response to the legitimate guilt and godly sorrow we feel from the proper understanding of the cross of Christ and the grace of God. After Peter preached the first Gospel message recorded in ACTS 2, the peoples' response was that *"they were cut to the heart and said to Peter and the other apostles, "Brothers, what shall we do?"* (ACTS 2:37)

Being cut to the heart shows that what was reasonable, the facts of Peter's message, reached the heart of the listeners which resulted in a search for the appropriate response and behavior. The realization of their guilt led them to a deeper level of humility and hunger for the truth.

Guilt and Shame

Though the words, "guilt" and "shame" are most often used synonymously. I use the two words in our discussion to make another important differentiation. Guilt in this case involves the feelings derived from wrong behavior, actions, attitudes, and thoughts of which we are in control. On the other hand, shame as used here involves negative feelings about who **we are** in contrast with what **we do**.

It is appropriate to have feelings of guilt associated with our sins and inappropriate to have feelings of shame over who we are. When someone is shamed the challenge is much deeper than a disappointment in behavior or even in one's character, because behavior and character can change.

Shame is a judgment on one's identity, a strike at the very legitimacy of one's being, a complete disregard for any value to a person's existence. It's fine and important to feel guilt about the wrong that we do, but it is never appropriate to feel shame about who we are.

We were born without sin and without a sinful nature. That's why Jesus used a child to define the essence of the heart we should have before God. Sin is a decision to think or act in a way that is against God's will (Matthew 18:3-4). When we sin, our sinful nature is born and continues with us for the rest of our lives. Jesus said, *"everyone who sins is a slave to sin."* (JOHN 8:34)

Even a causal look into the wonders of nature shows that God does not create something that he considers ugly, unfit, or without purpose. Particularly, if we have been created in his image as GENESIS 1:27 teaches.

Why is everything in the universe so meticulously and purposely designed and interwoven if not to convince us that God has a meticulous and defined purpose for each individual life? Why were we created to look, feel, and think differently from anyone else unless God had a purpose for each of our differences? So, if we were individually created from the mind of God for an eternal purpose, there is something to genuinely rejoice and find meaning in, and to pursue with all of our hearts.

Personal Worth and the Nothingness of Christ

The spiritual journey into the nothingness of Christ in no way implies we are no longer of any value or real worth to God— that somehow our worth is diminished the further we travel into this nothingness. To be "nothing" is not a valueless existence, but a state of mind from which true value and meaning can be ascertained. We should be thankful that we feel guilty about the sins we commit, that's where repentance begins, but we should always remember that we are a special part of God's creation.

This is the irony involved in becoming nothing. How can we possibly embrace this nothingness and still feel confident and secure about who we are in comparison to God? How can we be nothing and something of value at the same time? What else is there to hold onto when we become nothing? How do we wrap our emotions around two seemingly contradictory ideas?

Again, In order for these questions to be answered adequately, we must first be willing to allow God's view of us to define our view of ourselves. Without that commitment, we are left to the whims of our feelings which most often lead us away from a correct perspective of ourselves. God's feelings are the only ones that can be trusted fully.

If God says we were of value when created and are still worth much to him despite our sins, then we must work on letting that truth into the deepest parts of our hearts. And if becoming nothing opens our eyes to the realities of our true value and "somethingness" found only in Christ, then there is no contradiction at all, only the mysteriousness of God's work.

What helps us to trust that God is at work is not only to continue to grow in our realization of our nothingness before him, but also to deepen in our understanding and acceptance of the love of God. If we are not clear that the one who is leading us into the emptying process of humility really loves us, we will never trust the journey or the outcome. We all have probably played the game when we fell back into the arms of someone who catches us as a test of our faith. The key is to trust that the one catching you is capable and cares enough to break your fall.

On the journey to nothingness of Christ we must believe that we are falling back into the arms of a God who created the universe so he certainly has the power to catch us, and who also proved his love for us by allowing us to crucify his son for the forgiveness of our sins. If that is indeed the case and we aren't falling back, much about the message of Christ has still yet to be understood.

Self-Love and the Nothingness of Christ

And this is my prayer: that your love may abound more and more in knowledge and depth of insight, so that you may be able to discern what is best and may be pure and blameless for the day of Christ, filled with the fruit of righteousness that comes through Jesus Christ—to the glory and praise of God. (Philippians 1:9-11)

To mention the idea of the spiritual virtue, "nothingness," at first glance appears abstract and impractical. An idea for the gurus to contemplate in far-away incensed-filled mountain temples. Yet, Paul is not advocating life in a monastery or a depletion of one's life savings. The call is to a spiritual place much deeper than what can be achieved through isolation or payment. God is challenging our perspective about ourselves at a deep heart and intellectual level.

Yet, how do the practicalities of becoming "nothing" fit into a world in which achievement and success are so emphasized and prized, and in many cases necessary? Psychologists have realized for years the importance of self-acceptance or self-love as part of our emotional well-being and identity. Learning to love ourselves is key to a healthy spiritual experience, which in turn is partially a result of the success and achievement in life.

If we always feel like a failure, what is there to love about ourselves? And if we don't love ourselves, how will we be able to love others fully? We will be too self-consumed with our own pain. Jesus himself affirmed this when he commanded; *"Love your neighbor as yourself."* (Matthew 22:39) In other words, how we love ourselves will greatly affect the degree to which we can love others. If we have a poor self-image what are the chances of having a good image of others? If, out of insecurity, we live legalistic religious lives how then will we avoid the inappropriate unloving judgment we place on others?

All of us have a God-given drive for success and sense of achievement. Denying ourselves and living humbly for the sake of Christ should never be taken as an excuse for not expecting the best out of ourselves. The biblical emphasis on humility is not a promotion of vagrantness or vagabondism.

It is certainly appropriate for our need for success to reflect our own personal desire for spiritual progress and growth. Disciples of Christ want to grow spiritually and do our best for God, but often the lines are hard to distinguish between the desire to be **our** best and the desire to be **the** best. Perhaps at times they will be the same. Our best might well be the best. However, the upward climb to the best is not just an appropriate competition within ourselves but also often involves beating the outside competition — members of our family, friends, neighbors, and business colleagues.

This is where humility and gratitude are so essential. It helps to remember Paul's admonishment in PHILIPPIANS 2:3-4; *"Do nothing out of selfish ambition or vain conceit. Rather, in humility value others above yourselves, not looking to your own interests but each of you to the interests of the others."* If we receive a promotion, it means somebody else did not. Our joy is someone else's disappointment. Sometimes that can't be helped. We might well be the most qualified and deserve the promotion. And we should be grateful if we receive it. But, if in humility we consider the disappointment of others, valuing their feelings above our own, we have an opportunity to minister to others with the humility of Christ.

My father was a great model of humility for me. He was a very successful business man who retired as Senior Vice-President and member of the board of directors of a Fortune-500 company. He would arrive at his office in the executive suite an hour or more before work actually started, with the purpose of allowing those with lower positions in the company to talk with him—those who would never dare to enter the executive suite during normal hours—and to have access to a top executive to just talk.

My father told me they seldom talked about business but more so about their personal lives and families. Instead of flaunting his position and authority, he used his accomplishments as a means to serve others. He became "nothing" in order for others to feel a sense of being something.

As a spoiled clueless teenager, I saw no reason why dad would lose sleep just to talk with some lower-positioned employees. My identity-perspective was full of entitlement, egotism and complete delusion. How could I have ever thought I had any chance of an accurate opinion of the way my dad should conduct his business?

Another time I walked into the executive suite of offices looking for my dad and was redirected down a hall where all the offices looked the same. When I entered my dad's office I was shocked as I looked at him bent over a measly grey steel table. I said, "What on earth are you doing in this office?" He said, "Oh, they're doing some remodeling of the offices in the executive suite and we're restructuring executive responsibilities. I was asked to move down here for the time being." I remember feeling insulted and protective of my dad and said , "Why didn't they put one of the other guys down here? You're a Senior Vice-President and member of the board of directors. This office looks terrible for someone with your position!" As one raised during the Great Depression and who served as platoon leader during World War II, my dad looked at me with a smile and said, "Son, it's not about the kind of office a man is in, but what he does in the office."

I left scratching my head at the time, but realize now that was one of the most profound ideas he ever said to me. A humble man is grateful and free in his inner being to work and serve joyfully in any scenario whereas a prideful man is enslaved to his environment and position, and his own fear of loss.

Being the best does have its reassurances concerning confidence and ability. Yet, there is a sinister side to success that Jesus addresses when he stated, *"So the last will be first, and the first will be last."*(MATTHEW 20:16) Who exactly are the first and what does it mean to be last? What does being last have to do with being first? What are the eternal implications? The answers have everything to do with humility.

As I mentioned above, self-evaluation is important for spiritual growth but has to be exercised with great caution because of the dangerous potential our sense of progress has to become self-righteousness and arrogant. Any personal spiritual progress is due to God's power and intended to glorify him and not ourselves. James said, *"Every good and perfect gift is from above, coming down from the Father of the heavenly lights"* (JAMES 1:17) Paul had it right when he said, *"I can do all things through Christ who strengthens me."* (PHILIPPIANS 4:13). Christ is the source and reason for all of our spiritual success.

Paul's view of himself changed so that he no longer leaned on his past accomplishments for the confidence to deal with the conflicts in the ministry, but rather, on his faith in the power of Christ who would ultimately lead him to victory. Though his identity was under attack by the false teachers, his identity-perspective was firmly rooted in Christ. Spiritual success is achieved when we genuinely view our "worldly success" in this life as Paul did—nothing more than waste, in comparison to the success of knowing Christ and the spiritual power generated from the love of God, our love for ourselves and others, and from becoming nothing.

Am I affirming that all success is sinful? Should we take all of the diplomas and certificates of completion off the walls and rip up all of our resumes? Success is not the problem, but our emotional dependence on it is. If we allow the idea of success to identify us then success will become addictive and spiritually enslaving—a dependency on something which we cannot live happily without. Whether our success is real or only imagined, the drive for success can give birth to a delusion which shields us from the painful "owning" of life's failures. We somehow think that "success" will overshadow the reality of our sins.

It can even get to the point that when our failures become too overwhelming and our desperation for self-love too intense, our desire for success can lead us to lower our standards or to compare ourselves to those we deem less successful. The need to stay on top is critical to the insecure, even if only in one's deluded imagination.

There is nothing wrong about celebrating our own success when we achieve something we've worked hard for or to applaud the success of others. Jesus' first miracle was at a wedding celebration. Paul told Timothy that elders who direct the affairs of the church are worthy of double honor (1 TIMOTHY 5:17). We all want a surgeon with many successful surgeries to his credit and not one who has had only a few.

However, would we celebrate if one of our children, family, or friends decided to turn down a full scholarship to a prestigious university to relate better to the "uneducated" in order to win them to Christ? That is, to live with them and not "above" them. Would we judge their decision to result in a "missed opportunity"?

The truth is, many who have great aspirations for the education of their children would have a very difficult time with that decision. This is only one of many examples of the difficulty of applying the nothingness of Christ into our everyday decisions and letting it transform our perspective of who we really are and what our ultimate purpose is.

Jesus said it best when he stated in the Sermon on the Mount that if we do things to be seen, respected, or applauded by others, then we have received our reward in full (MATTHEW 6:1-18). If someone chooses a university primarily because of the prestige it carries with it, rather than, the glory it can bring to God, then the rewards associated with such prestige are certainly limited to this world. Whatever satisfaction comes from looking good in front of others is all the reward to be expected.

Some might ask, "Well, can't we become 'nothing' while we become 'something.'" What if God opens the door to an influential business position or an opportunity to join a prestigious club of some kind? What doors God opens for our lives is a personal matter between the individual and God. We just need to be confident that the door we see is a means to glorify God and not a door that fulfills a need for prominence, respect, or self-indulgence.

If we continue to fall prey to the temptation to allow our achievements to determine our identity and to become an emotional prop for our sense of self, then the journey downward into complete humility will have much greater challenges and is all the more difficult. The higher you go the harder it is to find your way down again.

Unfortunately, as we age we become more and more dependent on those possessions and people which and whom we believe determine our worldly and even spiritual security and success. The temptations can be strong to compromise our convictions in order to preserve our loyalty to a church, business, tradition, or a hierarchal church structure.

One of the greatest challenges to our identity-perspective is when we have to interact with those on whom we depend for our financial income or longevity in a position. Because we are so easily intimidated and impressed by the worldly and spiritual accomplishments of others, we fear distancing ourselves from them if we were to communicate and live by our own convictions. Incorporating self-love into our identity-perspective and centering our hopes on the eternal promises of Christ will help break the shackles from our need for prominence and the respect for others.

Here is the challenge. The journey of becoming nothing and the denial of self cannot be walked by those holding on to religious institutions, structures, and traditions, or who are overly concerned for the respect of others--but only by those willing to give up anything and everything to know Christ. A lot of people might tell you what Paul says in his letter to the Philippians, but Christ's nothingness can never receive an accurate interpretation unless the interpreter embraces the same experience. Paul said, "I want to know Christ." Not just knowledge about him, but him, all of him.

Grace and Sober Judgment

*For by the grace given me I say to every one of you: Do not think of yourself more highly than you ought, but rather think of yourself with **sober** judgment, in accordance with the faith God has distributed to each of you.* (ROMANS 12:3)

Paul teaches us to have a sober judgment of ourselves which is an admonition to apply God's objective view of us to our identity-perspectives. Though reaching sobriety spiritually can be an agonizing process, it is important to learn to live and feel comfortable with our true selves.

Some of the best actors in the world are personally very shy and insecure, yet find their confidence when acting like the character they are portraying. Unfortunately, that is not how to live life. It's sad when people feel more secure projecting someone other than who they really are, and are insecure being themselves.

Paul makes an important connection between grace and sober judgment. He said as quoted above, *"for by the grace given me . . ."* Without our acceptance of the grace of God, spiritual sobriety is impossible. One of the most terrifying parts of the journey into the nothingness of Christ is to take an honest look into our souls and be willing to embrace a true comparison of ourselves with God's ultimate perfection and power. Without the possibility of God's grace and mercy, that truth is too overwhelming to bear. Humanity cannot stand in the presence of a divine and perfect God. We should be thankful that God is perfect in his love as well as in all of his attributes.

God does not invite us to fellowship with him because of our success or earned entitlement to be in his presence, but rather, **because** of our humanity, weaknesses, and failures, and to give us that to which we have **no** entitlement. That is the grace of God. It is that grace that transforms us from being nothing to being something.

God's grace is undeserved and unearned and its power has no life on the field of success and pride. However, it blossoms on a field of failure and humility. That's what makes grace, grace. The grace of God enables us to embrace our true selves, which gives birth to the humility necessary to live life as Jesus did.

Grace provides the platform on which true honesty can take place. People are afraid to own their sins because they have no means of change, resolution, or atonement, and all they are left with are the raging feelings of guilt.

God enables us to be open and take responsibility for our failures because he provides the forgiveness we need in such a vulnerable state. The Apostle John puts it well in 1 JOHN 1; *"But if we walk in the light, as he is in the light, we have fellowship with one another, and the blood of Jesus, his Son, purifies us from all sin. If we confess our sins, he is faithful and just and will forgive us our sins and purify us from all unrighteousness."* (vss. 7, 9)

No one wants to be cut open in surgery unless the cutting has some hope of healing or preventing disease. With God, there is never only "some" hope, but always a guaranteed living hope. John said God will . . . *"purify us from **all** unrighteousness."* The deeper we internalize that truth, the more genuine and honest our openness will be.

Coming into the light and understanding how God views us ignites an important desperation to seek for solutions, the primary one being forgiveness from God. Jesus told this parable:

Two men went up to the temple to pray, one a Pharisee and the other a tax collector. The Pharisee stood by himself and prayed: 'God, I thank you that I am not like other people—robbers, evildoers, adulterers—or even like this tax collector. I fast twice a week and give a tenth of all I get.' But the tax collector stood at a distance. He would not even look up to heaven, but beat his breast and said, 'God, have mercy on me, a sinner.' I tell you that this man, rather than the other, went home justified before God. For all those who exalt themselves will be humbled, and those who humble themselves will be exalted. (LUKE 18:10-14)

Here we have a classic comparison between someone courageous enough to look inside and someone too afraid. Jesus is contrasting two identity-perspectives at opposite ends of the spectrum. The Pharisee's view of himself was muddied with deluded self-righteousness and biased comparison with others. There was no real gratitude for the mercy of God. There never is when righteousness is measured only by behavior.

The tax-collector, on the other hand, was beyond finding solace in his behavior. He was a "practicing" Jew like the Pharisee, both at the temple performing their religious acts; yet religious behavior did nothing to fill the emptiness in the tax-collector's heart, the hole left from a deep innate realization of the vast distance between traditional religious acts and the presence of God. The Pharisee took comfort in who he was not. The tax-collector desperately sought comfort from facing who he was. He exemplified what Jesus taught in MATTHEW 5:3; *"Blessed are the poor in spirit, for theirs is the kingdom of heaven."*

It's normal for Christians to be thankful that they have been able, through the power of God, to avoid the lifestyle and corruptive nature of the world. Yet, a change in heart and behavior does not change our core identity as sinners—redeemed sinners, but sinners nonetheless.

The Pharisee viewed himself to be in a separate category from all others—the root cause of disunity in the church. If other disciples are different from us we often avoid them, if a bit strange, we pity them, and if they're "struggling" or have emotional issues, we judge them.

The Pharisee never thought in terms of spiritual transformation, and therefore had no vision or hope for "sinners" who did not meet his approval. Tradition, prejudice, and ritualism fortified his iron-clad self-righteous judgment of others. There was no life worth living outside of his circle of Pharisaism.

Paul, a former Pharisee himself said, *"For I am the least of the apostles and do not even deserve to be called an apostle, because I persecuted the church of God. But by the grace of God I am what I am, and his grace to me was not without effect."* (1 CORINTHIANS 15:9-10) Paul regarded the mercy and grace of God as the primary influence on his identity-perspective.

Paul's willingness to acknowledge his total sinfulness allowed him to contently accept his standing among the other Apostles. His true identity was rooted in something much deeper than position and what others thought. Whether his perspective on his standing among the other Apostles was objective is not the point, but rather, how Paul was able to bring to nothingness his once passionate need and desire to be the most prominent.

It does not appear that his claim to be the least is from a negative and unhealthy self-image. This is not a victim's cry for pity. To be the "least" in heart opened the door to true greatness and the power of the grace of God in Paul's life. Among the "least," the "last" and the "weakest" is where the Kingdom of God on earth originated and where the power of God is most evident.

God's mercy had the amazing effect of transforming, energizing, and mobilizing Paul's heart; a heart that otherwise would have been consumed with legalism, pride, competitiveness, and hate. The grateful acceptance and understanding of God's grace allowed Paul to accept himself in spite of the full scope of his sin. It is not when the grace is given that ignites the power of God in our lives, but when the grace is accepted and internalized—when we are motivated to live as forgiven people. Gratitude for God's grace is empowered when we accept our nothingness before God.

To be the "least" is part of the journey and had become the main goal in Paul's life.

One of the greatest examples of self-denial and the abandonment of concern for personal identity is found in PHILIPPIANS 1:12-18.

> *Now I want you to know, brothers and sisters, that what has happened to me has actually served to advance the gospel. As a result, it has become clear throughout the whole palace guard and to everyone else that I am in chains for Christ. And because of my chains, most of the brothers and sisters have become confident in the Lord and dare all the more to proclaim the gospel without fear. It is true that some preach Christ out of envy and rivalry, but others out of goodwill. The latter do so out of love, knowing that I am put here for the defense of the gospel. The former preach Christ out of selfish ambition, not sincerely, supposing that they can stir up trouble for me while I am in chains. But what does it matter? The important thing is that in every way, whether from false motives or true, Christ is preached. And because of this I rejoice.*

The problem in the Philippian church involved the infiltration of "Christian" false teachers in the fellowship. These were teachers who emphasized the need for circumcision in order to be a "true" Christian. Paul strongly opposed the teaching and referred to the teachers as dogs, evildoers, and mutilators of the flesh (PHILIPPIANS 3:2).

Circumcision under the Old Law was an issue of identity. It identified one as a member of the Jewish nation. Having been *circumcised on the eighth day*, as Paul boosted about in his former life, (PHILIPPIANS 1:5) was of a particular significance because it was a sign of a genuine Israelite, as opposed to a circumcision performed on a convert to Judaism from a neighboring nation. Though allowed to participate in the Jewish sacrificial rites, converts to Judaism were still considered "low-class." It meant a lot to be a full-blooded Jew.

Paul's opposition to circumcision was not that it was an unhealthy surgical process but that it was being set forth theologically as a mark of one's true identity before God. Before the coming of Christ circumcision did identify one as part of the nation of Israel. However, with the coming of the Messiah a new definition of God's people made circumcision a meaningless procedure. "Circumcision" under Christ's teaching became a putting away of the sinful nature and no longer a removal of physical flesh.

> *In him you were also circumcised with a circumcision not performed by human hands. Your whole self ruled by the flesh was put off when you were circumcised by Christ, having been buried with him in baptism, in which you were also raised with him through your faith in the working of God, who raised him from the dead. When you were dead in your sins and in the uncircumcision of your flesh, God made you alive with Christ. He forgave us all our sins, . . .* (COLOSSIANS 2:11-13)

Although they accepted Jesus as the Messiah, the false teachers insisted that all Christians be circumcised physically in an attempt to keep Christianity within Jewish "borders" so to speak, closely associated with Jewish laws and customs. Paul did not have a problem with the "custom" side of things. In fact, because Timothy's father was Greek but his mother a Jew, Paul thought it best for Timothy to be circumcised because of the Jewish area where they were traveling. (ACTS 16:1-3) However, regarding Titus who was a Gentile, Paul refused to circumcise him because some made it an issue of salvation which Paul strongly opposed. (GALATIANS 2:1-5)

Amidst his imprisonment and the church issues involving circumcision and Paul's apostolic authority, Paul took hold of the opportunity to focus on incorporating his true objective identity of nothingness- before-God into his personal identity-perspective. By doing so he was able to subdue the emotional impact from his enemies' subjectively based and agenda-driven attacks.

There were two basic groups in the church, those who supported Paul and those who did not. However, both were preaching that Jesus is the Messiah, though his enemies were adding Jewish law to the Gospel message. The point here is that Paul was able to see beyond the complexities of the issues and find peace in the fact that Jesus was being preached regardless of all the in-fighting between the two groups. In the text quoted above from PHILIPPIANS 1:18 he stated, *"But what does it matter? The important thing is that in every way, whether from false motives or true, Christ is preached. And because of this I rejoice."*

In essence, Paul is saying, *"but what do I matter?"* That is the question we must always meditate upon. As long as our interests take precedence over all other interests we will never find meaningful resolution in our relationships. In the midst of controversy and relationship dysfunction this is an important question to ask. Why do you matter?

When discussing issues of principle, truth, and correct biblical interpretation, how much does position or self-perceived importance factor into the discussion? Often what seems as a fight for principle is, in reality, a fight because of the need to be right or vindicated, inflamed by competitiveness, insecurity, or even hate.

Paul could have taken the road to "somethingness" by brooding over the lack of respect shown to him as an Apostle or all of the false rumors circulated about him. In his second letter to the Corinthians he shares with us openly his struggles with such things. Instead here he shows in his inner identity-perspective he was able to remove himself from the arena of controversy, avoid bitterness, hate, and self-pity, while sitting back contently rejoicing that Jesus Christ was being preached as the Messiah. His mission of taking the name of Christ to the Gentile nations was being fulfilled even though Paul was confined to a prison cell. God indeed moves in mysterious ways

Chapter Four

HUMILITY: THE POWER BEHIND FAITH AND LOVE

I thank my God every time I remember you. In all my prayers for all of you, I always pray with joy because of your partnership in the gospel from the first day until now, being confident of this, that he who began a good work in you will carry it on to completion until the day of Christ Jesus. It is right for me to feel this way about all of you, since I have you in my heart and, whether I am in chains or defending and confirming the gospel, all of you share in God's grace with me. God can testify how I long for all of you with the affection of Christ Jesus. (PHILIPPIANS 1:3-8)

One of the results of moving toward a more complete self-denial is the ability to love more genuinely and fully even in very intense relationship disagreements. It is important to recognize the background of the book of Philippians to be a church in serious turbulence. In his absence, Paul was being undermined by teachers whom he refers to as "dogs" and "mutilators of the flesh" (those of the circumcision group) There were "brothers" who disagreed with Paul on the issue of circumcision and the application of the Old Law and in turn used Paul's imprisonment as an opportunity to promote and confirm their position. From the world's perspective Paul had good reason to be offended, bitter, and hateful.

Where does someone find the faith and love to have vision for people who never seem to know which side to stand on? Where does the power come from to take the high road even in relationships with extreme personality dissimilarities and conflicts?

Paul had already expended so much physical and emotional energy for the sake of these churches. What chance did a letter have against such emotionalism, confusion, ignorance, and rampant self-promotion? Yet, because of his ability to love in a challenging situation, Paul held on to the hope that if the Philippians could find the resolve to follow his teaching they would again find their way. *"Love . . . always hopes, always perseveres."* (1 CORINTHIANS 13:7)

With the example of Jesus' humility on his heart, Paul was able to understand the distinction between the content of the attacks against him and the real issues causing the rampant disunity. Spiritual discernment is never achieved in self-affirmation. The battle wasn't all about him. He said, *"I have been crucified with Christ and I no longer live, but Christ lives in me"* (Galatians 2:20). Embracing the identity of Christ allowed Paul to experience contentment in a very troubling situation.

Paul embraced the objective nothingness of his true identity before God—a servant of God and nothing more, no chip on his shoulder and nothing personally to prove. Because he was a sinner he understood he was not entitled to any love from the Philippians, or anybody else, for that matter. He deserved nothing. He was a merely a servant of the Christ with a mission. God's love for him was enough. Whatever love he did receive, if only from a few, was more than he deserved and was greatly appreciated and motivating.

Even in the midst of all of the congregational turmoil Paul captured a memory of love and relationship. It was the refreshing and empowering experience of love in spite of so much hate, distrust, and conflict that provided the motivation to persevere. When someone really loves, perseverance is a foregone conclusion.

Jesus and the "Sinful Woman"

A great example of the relationship between humility, faith, and love is recorded in LUKE 7:36-50. Simon, a Pharisee, invited Jesus to have dinner at his house along with some other guests. While dining, a woman who lived a "sinful" life, probably a life of prostitution, entered the house uninvited and stood behind Jesus weeping. As her tears fell on Jesus' feet, she knelt down and wiped his feet with her hair and rubbed them with the perfume she had brought with her.

As the blind man in JOHN 9 discussed above, this woman was anything but respected in the world in which she lived. A life for her was quite unlike the lifestyle of a high-class Las Vegas call girl. As most prostitutes in the world, one can only imagine the emotional trauma, physical and sexual abuse, and lack of self-acceptance she must have faced in her life.

Women in the first century were often regarded overall as nothing more than property. As in many parts of the world today, physical and sexual abuse were not against the law. Once a woman's usefulness or attraction wore out, women could be divorced and left to fend for themselves. If there were no opportunities for remarriage women had few options to make a living. One of these options was prostitution.

This woman stood in the presence of the Son of God weeping as the other guests were undoubtedly conversing about the many issues of religion, politics, and everyday life. Why she was weeping we can only conjecture, but it would appear she had reached the point of nothingness with nowhere else to go. The glares of the judgmental Pharisees were not having the same effect as times past and did nothing to squelch her determination to express her love through her tears and wiping Jesus' feet. Humility develops our character to withstand the legalistic judgments of others.

The glares and thoughts of Simon the Pharisee caused Jesus to cite a parable in which two men owed a money lender different amounts, one was much higher than the other. The moneylender cancelled both of their debts. Jesus asked Simon a rhetorical question regarding who would love the moneylender more. Obviously, the man who had the greater debt, Simon replied. (LUKE 7:43)

Our gratitude for God's acceptance of us in spite of our sin is the foundation for our love for him — the deeper our gratitude the deeper and more genuine our love. Out of her desperation from recognizing her true self — a life of shame, guilt, and abuse — this woman was humbled and courageous to love no matter what the risks were to her reputation and name. All of that concern had faded because of the ravages of sin, and she had nothing else but an alabaster jar of perfume and the love in her heart to give to Jesus. Humility allows us to go places that the prideful cannot access.

This shows once again how important identity-perspective is to our hope for forgiveness. Notice the progression of spiritual growth in the prostitute. First, we see a humility carved out of the "hard living" of prostitution, and then a faith and love powerful enough to enable this woman to endure the most humiliating of circumstances. This, in turn resulted in a faith strong enough to stand in the presence of the Son of God. The Pharisaical bubble from which Simon viewed life blinded him from the reality of his spiritual state, which ironically was no different than the woman's. She was willing to see, and he wasn't. She went home forgiven, he went home lost.

Jesus commended the woman for faith and does not mention her humility because humility is implied any time true faith is present. The Pharisees' identity-perspectives were contaminated with religious traditions and self-righteousness, and the delusion that somehow they were people of prominence because they were having dinner with someone in the social and religious spotlight. Focusing on Jesus' prominence rather than his heart and humility, the Pharisees failed to appreciate the ease with which Jesus connected with "sinners." They were looking through a stain-glassed window at the Son of God, unable to get a clear perspective of themselves and the true identity of Jesus of Nazareth.

The different emotions and thoughts present at the dinner are too numerous to discuss. Some were undoubtedly torn between their fear of being seen with Jesus and their fear of turning down the invitation to meet the famous carpenter's son. What if Jesus was the Messiah? They would have missed a great occasion with incredible political possibilities and bragging opportunities for the rest of their lives.

Yet, if Jesus was only an astute rebel as many believed, then being connected to him in any way could have dire consequences. Others at the dinner were probably afraid to speak up because they had heard of Jesus' expertise at debate and silencing his questioners. At the end of it all, it appears all that Simon and his guests saw was what they perceived as incompetency on the part of a so-called prophet unable to determine what type of people he allowed to touch him.

This "sinful" woman represents everything our identity-perspective needs to be, kneeling with tears at the feet of Jesus with all we own being laid at his feet. If our spiritual "experiences" are not preceded by a deep transformation in our view of ourselves the experiences will do nothing more than add to the misguided perception of being right with God.

Jesus and the Canaanite Woman

Leaving that place, Jesus withdrew to the region of Tyre and Sidon. A Canaanite woman from that vicinity came to him, crying out, "Lord, Son of David, have mercy on me! My daughter is demon-possessed and suffering terribly." Jesus did not answer a word. So his disciples came to him and urged him, "Send her away, for she keeps crying out after us." He answered, "I was sent only to the lost sheep of Israel." The woman came and knelt before him. "Lord, help me!" she said. He replied, "It is not right to take the children's bread and toss it to the dogs." "Yes it is, Lord," she said. "Even the dogs eat the crumbs that fall from their master's table." Then Jesus said to her, "Woman, you have great faith! Your request is granted." And her daughter was healed at that moment. (MATTHEW 15:21-28)

When I first read this passage after I became a Christian, it seemed that Jesus was insensitive, rude, and even racist in dealing with this woman. In order to understand what Jesus was doing some historical background discussion is necessary.

The societal borders concerning religious customs and traditions were tight around first-century Judaism, and whatever benevolent obligation the Jews felt was most often directed to the needy within the Jewish community. The cries of the Canaanite woman did little to conjure up any feelings of moral obligation among the disciples.

Jewish theocratic tradition taught that non-Jewish people were unclean because of the lack of circumcision, dietary differences, and the various gods they worshipped. Not only was this person non-Jewish, but a woman as well. There were very strict traditions in the Jewish community regarding the role of men and women and how they were expected to relate to one another, particularly in public.

Jesus had no real obligation to even talk to the woman, particularly a non-Jewish woman, which is probably why he initially said nothing in response to her cries for help. He was using the religious and social customs to test the level of this woman's humility and love and to teach his disciples an important lesson about genuine faith.

After the disciples' anxious reactions to the awkwardness of the situation, Jesus told the woman he was sent only to the lost sheep of Israel. With this statement Jesus highlighted the Jewish-Gentile wall that existed in the first century, the understanding that the Messiah would only be a deliverer for Israel, to protect her from the nations around her. Non-Jewish people were not considered to have any rights to the Messiah's protection, leadership, or miraculous blessings.

The love this woman had for her daughter enabled her to overcome any personal concerns for her dignity and self-respect — whether or not she felt accepted, included, or personally valuable in the presence of the Lord.

Love is a powerful force which melts away what seems like insurmountable odds. Her willingness to undergo intense racial scrutiny and bigotry along with the trauma of her helpless situation, revealed her deep faith in the power of humility.

The healing power that she heard Jesus possessed was the only option she had left. Her love for her daughter pushed her forward. Jesus' reference to her as a "dog," using the local Jewish perspective, was the height of his challenge to her. She undoubtedly stood at the crossroads between allowing insult to wound her so deeply to turn her slithering back into the crowd; or allowing her nothingness to absorb the insult enabling her to respond with a statement of humility and faith.

What appears to be racial bigotry on the part of Jesus was a preconceived plan to hold up this woman as a classic example of faith. Jesus was on his way to give his life for the sins of the world and expected the Gospel to be preached by the disciples to all the nations (MATTHEW 28:18). So, racism was not in the heart of Christ.

This woman's identity-perspective and the power of love in the midst of nothingness were exemplary. In spite of all the cultural prejudices against her, the glares of judgment and disgust, she kept pursuing Jesus to heal her daughter. Unabashed by the insults, she responded that even the dogs eat the crumbs that fall from the table. With this response, Jesus congratulated the women on her faith and healed her daughter.

Honesty with ourselves is paramount if there is to be any applicable meaning of this passage in our lives. If we were one of the Jewish disciples standing with Jesus while this woman cried out, our reactions would have been the same—disgust, prejudice, embarrassment, and the desire to send this woman away. It's much easier to remove the object of our disgust than it is to remove the disgusting bigotry in our hearts.

It is important to note that the reason the Gospel writers mention so often Jesus' ministry to Gentile "outsiders" is to show that the Kingdom of God has a new definition. It was no longer to be defined by position, exclusion, legalism, and clearly defined land borders, but by the last becoming first and the first last—where the ideal is the heart of a child and servanthood is the greatest achievement of all.

Chapter Five

SUFFERING AND CHRIST'S HUMILITY

I want to know Christ — yes, to know the power of his resurrection and participation in his sufferings, becoming like him in his death, and so, somehow, attaining to the resurrection from the dead. (PHILIPPIANS 3:10-11)

I f God is so loving, compassionate, and powerful, why is there so much suffering in the world? Why is there any suffering at all? There doesn't seem to be any suffering in heaven so why so much suffering in our world? This question has been set forth by the advocates of atheism since the Enlightenment for well over a century. The attack is not as much on the power of God as it is on the Christian teaching that God is a benevolent God. The existence of suffering is a challenge to the moral fiber of God's character. Why would a benevolent and kind God allow such things as genocide, disease, physical and mental disabilities, and infant suffering?

The truth is much of the suffering in the world involves the evil that people do to one another and is a result of a person's will and not God's. Even beyond the physical harm we cause, is the emotional damage and shame that we inflict on each other. Yet, why would God allow somebody to inflict suffering on someone else? Doesn't he have the power to protect each individual?

Atheists maintain there are only two choices—that God either does not have the power or he is not a loving God. According to them, either one undermines the existence of a Christian God. They believe they have the idea of our God backed into a corner.

Yet, there is another option to consider, and that is divine purpose. In other words, the question is; is it possible that suffering is necessary for our identity-perspective to be that of a servant, a follower of a suffering Messiah? If following Christ is our passion and heaven our ultimate goal, then does not the reality of temporary suffering pale in comparison to the realities of eternal life? Paul apparently thought so when he said: *"I consider that our present sufferings are not worth comparing with the glory that will be revealed in us."* (ROMANS 8:18)

Since none of us has personally stood in the presence of God, any comparison from actual experience between the "glory" that we have coming and the sufferings is impossible. But, in any comparison between life in the temporal and eternal realms, isn't it reasonable that the eternal realm should be our primary concern? And if so, how can we possibly argue that temporary sufferings could not possibly be part of God's plan to get us to heaven? Particularly, as we have discussed, when we understand how crucial suffering is to the development of humility, which ultimately determines where we spend eternity. We are, therefore, not victims of suffering but products of its chiseling.

The book of Job in the Old Testament is a classic look at the problem of suffering. God allowed Job to be tested with disease and the loss of children and assets. Because of his suffering friends of Job doubted his righteousness before God which led

Job to question the purpose of suffering. God responded to Job's ignorance by turning the tables and questioning him:

> "Will the one who contends with the Almighty correct him? Let him who accuses God answer him!" . . . "Brace yourself like a man; I will question you, and you shall answer me." Would you discredit my justice? Would you condemn me to justify yourself? Do you have an arm like God's, and can your voice thunder like his? Then adorn yourself with glory and splendor, and clothe yourself in honor and majesty. Unleash the fury of your wrath, look at all who are proud and bring them low, look at all who are proud and humble them, crush the wicked where they stand. Bury them all in the dust together; shroud their faces in the grave. Then I myself will admit to you that your own right hand can save you. (JOB 40:2, 7-14)

God is asking Job to demonstrate something to show the wisdom of his opposition to any rational explanation for suffering. God is challenging Job to come up with a better means to humble and bring low the proud. If pride is the primary sin which separates us from God and from which all other sins emerge, then what is Job's plan for helping the prideful overcome their sin? If he has no other alternative, then on what basis does he have for criticizing God's use of suffering to that end?

We have all either been or have known someone who at one time was prideful, arrogant, and self-centered, yet who because of physical pain or a deep sense of hopelessness became humble, caring, and other-centered. Humility is a prerequisite to having a relationship with God. If suffering can be shown to help someone in the surrendering process, then is it not justified?

If we react to the **degree** of suffering in the world then there are a couple of ideas to consider. First of all, the idea of suffering is loosely and subjectively defined. What is suffering for one person might not be suffering for the next. There are too many examples to mention, but one might help illustrate the point. The rain forests of Brazil with their hot and steamy climate, poisonous snakes and insects would be intense suffering for someone from Montana but not for a native of that region.

We, as Humankind, are all incredibly adaptable to our environments, from the bitter cold of northern Russia to the stifling heat of the Sahara desert. God made us with the ability to adapt. No matter how extreme the conditions there are always people who know nothing else, have learned to adapt, and are actually quite content in their environment. In those circumstances the degree of suffering might need to be more intense if God's intentions for suffering are fulfilled.

We struggle with the problem of suffering in the world because we evaluate others' experiences through our own lens. We need to embrace the reality that because of God's power, omniscience, and love, he is working in each individual life in ways beyond our ability to comprehend.

Jesus taught in the last part of MATTHEW 6, that even the hairs of our heads are numbered, and a sparrow does not fall from the sky without God knowing about it. Jesus referred to the beauty and splendor of the lilies in the field, then stressed the value and beauty of each human life. If God is involved with birds and flowers we can rest assured he is more concerned about us.

As we discussed above, if we understand God to have created the universe out of nothing and if he has demonstrated his ability to heal suffering as he did through the ministry of Jesus Christ, then God's power is not the issue. And if one understands the theology of a crucified Christ, then the love of God is also not the issue. All of us need to work on growing in our faith in a loving creator. If God can create from nothing, then he can remove from existence anything in the creation. So if God decides **not** to remove suffering there must be a loving purpose behind it. That is, if we believe that God is love.

The Apostle Paul and Suffering

Paul's life as an Apostle offers great insight into the importance of suffering for our journey to the humility of Christ. We see an example of someone deeply committed to following Christ but with still much to learn about humility and dependence on God.

Paul had the unique calling to be the Apostle who would be known throughout history for the suffering he would endure. When Ananias was sent by God to restore Paul's sight and baptize him, Ananias questioned the Lord about the wisdom of that decision. The Lord responded; *"Go! This man is my chosen instrument to proclaim my name to the Gentiles and their kings and to the people of Israel. I will show him how much he must suffer for my name."* (ACTS 9:15-16) In other words, Paul was to be the "Job" to his generation.

In 2 CORINTHIANS 1:8-9, Paul writes; *"We do not want you to be uninformed, brothers and sisters about the troubles we experienced in the province of Asia. We were under great pressure, far beyond our ability to endure, so that we despaired of life itself. Indeed, we felt we had received the sentence of death. But this happened that we might not rely on ourselves but on God, who raises the dead."*

Suffering has a purpose—to help transform our identify-perspective, deepen our reliance on God, and help us understand our objective physical nothingness before him. Notice the verbiage; *We were under great pressure, far beyond our ability to endure, so that we despaired of life itself.* Paul was led into an experience which took him beyond his physical and emotional abilities of endurance. Through the ordeal he was more convinced of his need for God and describes God as a deliverer. Suffering had become Paul's "burning bush"—where he stood in the presence of God.

What would you do if you found yourself hanging over the Grand Canyon on a rope that was slowly breaking and God reached down and offered you his hand? Of course, you would grab it. But what state of mind would cause you to do so? Would you reach out because of the comfort or the desperation of your situation? The more desperate our experiences are, the tighter our grip on God's hand will be.

It's difficult to cite one biblical character who grew in their faith in God any other way. Adam was thrown out of the garden, Noah spent decades building an ark, Abraham was told to sacrifice his son, Moses was called to lead a wandering nation of rebellious people, David spent years living in caves, John the Baptist lived in the desert, and Jesus became human.

Another passage which holds much insight into the spiritual purposes for suffering is 2 CORINTHIANS 12:7-10:

> *Therefore, in order to keep me from becoming conceited, I was given a thorn in my flesh, a messenger of Satan, to torment me. Three times I pleaded with the Lord to take it away from me. But he said to me, "My grace is sufficient for you, for my power is made perfect in weakness." Therefore I will boast all the more gladly about my weaknesses, so that Christ's power may rest on me. That is why, for Christ's sake, I delight in weaknesses, in insults, in hardships, in persecutions, in difficulties. For when I am weak, then I am strong.*

The context of this passage involves the fact that Paul *"was caught up to paradise and heard inexpressible things, things that no one is permitted to tell."* (2 CORINTHIANS 12:4) In light of this incredible revelation, Paul was given a "thorn" in his flesh, serious enough for him to plead with God three times to have it removed. His requests were denied with God's response, *"My grace is sufficient for you, for my power is made perfect in weakness."* (vs. 9) Paul needed to understand more deeply the power of God's grace — that there is much more to be attained in life than comfort and freedom from suffering. Growth in our dependence on God is the goal no matter what the catalyst.

Whatever Paul's thorn was, God considered it essential to Paul's spiritual journey. After contemplating the gift of God's grace in the midst of his suffering, Paul was able to say; *"Therefore I will boast all the more gladly about my weaknesses, so that Christ's power may rest on me. That is why, for Christ's sake, I delight in weaknesses, in insults, in hardships, in persecutions, in difficulties. For when I am weak, then I am strong."* (vss. 9-10)

As we discussed above, God by nature is powerful. Powerful enough to create something from nothing and powerful enough to remove thorns in people's lives. However, God is also by nature love and considers our eternal well-being more important than the suffering we so intensely resist and the freedom from suffering we so earnestly seek.

Notice the wording, *"to keep me from becoming conceited."* The thorn was given to Paul to insure he stayed on the right path. It goes to show that Humankind just can't handle the miraculous. We run from it, deny it, give ourselves the credit for it, or get enslaved to the constant need for it. People flock to "Holy Places" and various sites world-wide where some silhouette or image of the Virgin Mary or Jesus Christ seems to have appeared; or they attend religious meetings and conferences with the hope that perhaps the time has come for them to receive their personal miracle. They fail to see the miraculous all around them. Paul's thorn was part of a miraculous plan to transform his heart and keep his eyes open to miraculous work of God in every facet of his existence.

To confirm the Gospel message in the first century, many were given the miraculous gifts of healing, knowledge, and a host of other gifts. Yet, the disunity, conceit, and factions within the Corinthian church over which gift-holder should be considered the most prominent shows how we fumble the miraculous every time it's thrown to us. Instead of the miraculous bringing the Corinthians to a greater sense of awe of God and church unity, they became more in awe of themselves — the exact opposite of humility.

Paul was exposed to *inexpressible things*. One would think that would be enough to keep him humble and convinced of his nothingness before God. Apparently, however, it was more likely that Paul's identity-perspective would turn to his own greatness, rather than his nothingness in the presence of the greatness of God. God loved him enough to keep that from happening and gave him the "gift" of a thorn in the flesh.

Paul's experience with suffering was ever-present, intended to keep him on his journey to self-denial, and to serve as a universal witness of how important physical weakness is to our spiritual focus and growth. Every disciple would love to have Paul's spiritual perspective on existence, but very few would relish the experience that produced that perspective. The opportunity to continue to grow in his knowledge of God through suffering brought Paul to express, *I want to know Christ . . . and participation in his sufferings, becoming like him in his death . . .* (PHILIPPIANS 3:10)

We understand this principle when it involves athletic achievement and development. "No pain, no gain" is the well-known slogan. Athletes endure months and even years of grueling and painful training in order to achieve success in their various sports. Pain to an athlete triggers the motivation to persevere because of the physical rewards that lay ahead. Suffering to the disciple of Christ should trigger an excitement that motivates us to push through a painful experience to learn the deeper lessons that come only through difficult experiences.

Whatever the origins of our suffering might be, whether it is health issues, abusive spouses, family deaths and problems, or financial strains, no one comes to God until they have exhausted their abilities to endure, and despair of living a solution-less life of constant pressure and inner turmoil. This is how God draws us to him. Jesus said, *"No one can come to me unless the Father who sent me draws them. . ."* (JOHN 6:44) We must trust the drawing power of a loving God.

Suffering and Victory over Sin

Therefore, since Christ suffered in his body, arm yourselves also with the same attitude, because whoever suffers in the body is done with sin. As a result, they do not live the rest of their earthly lives for evil human desires, but rather for the will of God. (1 PETER 4:1-2)

In this passage the Apostle Peter admonished his readers to imitate Jesus' attitude — to arm themselves with a mindset capable of withstanding intense temptations in the most challenging arenas of our existence — the arena of human suffering.

Normally, we regard suffering as the source for most of our sin, which is why the cross was the ultimate and final test of Jesus' commitment. Yet, here Peter sets forth suffering as the reason for our victory over sin.

At first glance it appears that Peter is emphasizing the finality of sin in our lives. If we will but suffer in the body we will be *"done with sin,"* as he puts it. That is true if we are willing to suffer and resist sin to the extent that Jesus suffered and resisted. Yet, that is the ideal and should not be interpreted to say that there will ever be a time in this life when we will no longer have to battle and overcome sin. Rather, embracing and enduring suffering for the sake of righteousness refines our faith and deepens our commitment to deal with our sin. Suffering and victory over sin have a very close relationship.

The challenge is that the refinement of our faith includes fiery trials. Peter said in regard to these trials, *"These have come so that the proven genuineness of your faith—of greater worth than gold, which perishes even though refined by fire—may result in praise, glory and honor when Jesus Christ is revealed."* (1 PETER 1:7)

The issue here for most disciples is not whether we **ought** to have the attitude of Christ, and joyfully accept whatever life throws at us, but more so, how to implement such an attitude. Jesus is clear that he is to be our standard for all that we think and do. As his disciples, we all confessed that he is Lord of our lives. But during experiences of extreme physical and emotional suffering, how do we imitate someone so perfect, so relentless in conviction, with an over-the-top passion for prayer, and complete dependence on God?

Without the same experiences of suffering it is difficult to know exactly what in our attitudes needs to change. How do we know if we're prepared for intense experiences unfamiliar to many Christians today?

To begin to answer that question, we would do well to look at some of the specifics of Christ's attitude while he suffered. Peter says:

> To this you were called, because Christ suffered for you, leaving you an example, that you should follow in his steps. "He committed no sin, and no deceit was found in his mouth." When they hurled their insults at him, he did not retaliate; when he suffered, he made no threats. Instead, he entrusted himself to him who judges justly. (1 PETER 2:21-23)

That we have been called to suffer must become part of our identity. Not just an occasional experience but something that we willingly accept as part of a mindset and an important means through which we identify with the being of Christ. Just as Jesus was the "Suffering Messiah," we must view ourselves as the "suffering servants" of the Messiah. This is our new identity in Christ.

Embracing all aspects of our new identity with a grateful and willing heart is foundational to arming ourselves with the proper attitude. If we are not grateful for what we have been called to be we certainly won't be grateful for the journey ahead. In order not to be blindsided by persecution or suffering some discussion regarding the area of "expectations" might be helpful. What we expect out of life has a lot to do with our ability to endure whatever comes our way.

There are three categories of expectations I believe are important to consider. The first is what I call "accepted expectations." These are expectations that we not only expect but also accept—the kind when we have had sufficient time to contemplate and surrender to the task ahead. Surrender is an important virtue and has everything to do with overcoming the temptations associated with suffering.

If we do not surrender to God's expectation for our lives, then we will never be able to joyfully accept what we have been called to be. The challenge is to surrender our will and gratefully and humbly accept the will of God, whatever the circumstances, hardship, or suffering. We expect to suffer and we are grateful for the opportunity to have our faith refined.

For the most part we are better able to deal with a difficult situation if it is something we expect to happen. For example, when we anticipate a busy difficult day at work, it is easier to undergo the hardship because of our prior expectation and emotional preparation.

There was never a time in the mind of Christ when he was without the expectation that he would suffer while in human form. He never resisted, complained, or allowed self-pity to enter his heart. It was his decision to deny himself and become human. Humbly accepting God's expectations for his life was the key to enduring his destiny of suffering.

Many appear to be living a life of "nothingness" because of the poverty or meager circumstances in which they live. Yet, the essence of living by the principles of the nothingness of Christ is the grateful, joyful acceptance of those circumstances, and not just enduring what might be considered less-than-desirable surroundings.

Endurance is a given if one's circumstances cannot change; what other options are there? It's like a prison guard locking an inmate in his cell and saying "Stay here." The question is what kind of person are we becoming while we endure — bitter, full of self-pity, self-centered, discontent, or preferably, more dependent on God, grateful, and full of anticipation for the coming glory?

The second category of expectations involves "unfilled expectations." These are the expectations people have, whether realistic or not, that never come to fruition. It is normal as we mature as adults to readjust our expectations for ourselves and other people, but there are many expectations that run deep throughout our identity-perspective — those that involve much more than what we envision ourselves owning or even achieving, but expectations about who we are or want to be.

When people don't meet their personal expectations, it normal to flounder spiritually, become guilt-ridden, hopeless, and passionless. We lose heart and find ourselves reaching for the stars, but never able to get above the trees.

The third category of expectations concerns "unexpected expectations." These are on-the-spot expectations which come out of nowhere, but carry the pressure of needing to be fulfilled. These are the hardest expectations to endure because we usually don't have time to adjust our attitude. It is much easier to deal with hardship when we know what to expect. We most often resist the unexpected.

I saw this dynamic when dealing with my children when they were young. We were often invited to other families' home and the children would play with each other while the adults visited. When it was time to go, we would go through the normal whining and the children's attempts to negotiate and manipulate for a longer time to play.

What I learned was that I was not giving my children enough time to accept the reality that it was indeed time to leave. So, about a half-hour before it was time to leave I would start my departure strategy by telling the children we would be leaving in a few moments. After about 15 minutes I would tell them again, and then after another 10 minutes, so that when I announced it was time to go, the resistance was minimal if any.

Unfortunately, as adults we have the same tendency to whine and grumble when we are faced with unexpected responsibilities, particularly those which add stress and suffering. If we do not arm ourselves with the proper identity-perspective — that of being suffering servants — and the willingness to joyfully step up to all aspects of our suffering, we will fall prey to the temptations of bitterness, doubt, self-pity, and cowardice.

Take the Apostle Peter for an example. Though a man of conviction and passion, during the trial of Jesus he was caught off guard by a young girl standing by the fire who recognized his accent and accused him of being one of Jesus' disciples. Peter had previously pledged to Jesus that he would go to prison and death with him, and viewed himself as brave and ready to take on whatever challenges following Jesus brought to him.

It is one thing to commit yourself to going to prison and to death with someone who demonstrated the power to heal, resurrect, and calm a dangerous storm; and quite another to be willing to suffer and die alone. Peter intellectually knew that there were to be great spiritual battles in front of him and that his courage would be tested, but never expected the test to begin with the accusations of a peasant girl. A girl who was obviously a "nobody" with little more than nothing, brought the great Apostle to his knees. Peter thought he was ready to face suffering, yet was exposed by God as being anything but ready.

Jesus stood spiritually victorious through the ordeal of his trial and crucifixion because he fully expected and accepted that death would be the fulfillment of his mission as the Son of Man. He never resisted, grumbled, or complained. Consider the contents of these two quotations:

> *In the beginning was the Word, and the Word was with God, and the Word was God. He was with God in the beginning. Through him all things were made; without him nothing was made that has been made.* (JOHN 1:1-3)

> *In the past God spoke to our ancestors through the prophets at many times and in various ways, but in these last days he has spoken to us by his Son, whom he appointed heir of all things, and through whom also he made the universe.* (HEBREWS 1:1-2)

According to the Gospel of John and the book of Hebrews Jesus was the agent of God's creation, and therefore it was he who created the human body with pain receptacles in the brain and nerves extending throughout the entire body. Jesus was part of creating the very body he was to occupy. So he knew full well what to expect. His decision to save us included his decision to suffer.

Christians must have the attitude of "accepted expectations." We should have the expectation that at times in our lives we will need to suffer because of our relationship with God. Our example and Lord was a poor carpenter's son, persecuted, misrepresented, flogged, beaten, and crucified on a cross in poverty. Suffering was the reason the disciples fled Christ's crucifixion. In light of the multitude of healings Jesus performed while with them, the suffering of Jesus was far from any of their expectations and thus too much to accept at the time.

Long after the Apostle Peter's repentance from cowardice he said, *"But if you suffer for doing good and you endure it, this is commendable before God. To this you were called, because Christ suffered for you, leaving you an example, that you should follow in his steps"* (1 PETER 2:20-21). That is about the clearest definition of the crux of the Christian life. No whining or grumbling, just following and being thankful that suffering is helping us stay on the right road.

Sadly, many buy into a theological perspective that teaches that God is there to take care of all of our worldly needs. There is the assumption that the deeper our faith the more we will receive—freedom from suffering, miraculous healing of our physical ailments, and financial prosperity.

A deep faith does have its rewards. But the real rewards of faith involve not the removal of suffering or poverty from our lives but the transformation of our perspective in life's difficult circumstances. The Apostle Peter said:

> *This inheritance is kept in heaven for you, who through faith are shielded by God's power until the coming of the salvation that is ready to be revealed in the last time. In all this you greatly rejoice, though now for a little while you may have had to suffer grief in all kinds of trials. These have come so that the proven genuineness of your faith—of greater worth than gold, which perishes even though refined by fire—may result in praise, glory and honor when Jesus Christ is revealed.* (1 PETER 1:4-7)

Faith provides us access to the protection of God's power. But the practical question is, protection from what? Peter did not predict that the trials would miraculously end. He does promise a refined faith would come out of the trials, but not necessarily a decrease in their intensity.

The only means by which trials can be minimized is through our perspective of them. The intensity of any trial is largely controlled by our faith—the ability to "see through" our present suffering into the eternal truths that determine our destiny. Our faith certainly ignites the possibility of the "miraculous" in our lives, but the real miracle is the transformation of our faith.

All of our spiritual expectations cannot center on the blessings in this life. When suffering stays longer than expected many lose their faith because it was rooted in this life and not the next. There was never a time in the identity-perspective of Christ that he did not view himself as the "Suffering Messiah." A Suffering Messiah destined to sit once again at the right hand of God.

The Jewish people had anticipated the coming of the Messiah for centuries. But never in their wildest imagination would he suffer and die on a cross. That was part of an identity-perspective set on false hopes of what the Messiah could do for them and not on how they should serve and worship him. They viewed themselves as the "receivers" of God's blessings, and not as his agents through which the message of Christ would be preached to all the nations.

Until the Valleys and Mountaintops Become One

Rejoice in the Lord always. I will say it again: Rejoice! Let your gentleness be evident to all. The Lord is near. Do not be anxious about anything, but in every situation, by prayer and petition, with thanksgiving, present your requests to God. And the peace of God, which transcends all understanding, will guard your hearts and your minds in Christ Jesus. (PHILIPPIANS 4:4-7)

Because of life's disappointments—pain, death of loved ones, heartache, betrayal by those we put our trust and hope in—we can often feel like we are on an emotional elevator never knowing what floor to get off on. We all recognize that life will be filled with ups and downs, mountaintop and valley experiences, as they say. But the experience itself is daunting.

Everyone loves the mountaintops where contentment and the true realization of the grace of God are found. Our reactions to the valleys are another matter altogether—times when depression, physical and emotional pain, hopelessness, and loss take their toll. However, for the mountaintops to be truly appreciated the valleys must also be appreciated because it is only the valleys that give meaning to the mountaintops. Learning to be joyful in hope and grateful in victory is the only way to fulfill Paul's admonition to rejoice in the Lord always. Did Paul mean to rejoice only during times of prosperity and well-being?

It is in the valley of despair where God molds our earthen vessels from the inside out. Hard times are the only way spiritual character is molded. Notice Paul's words in Romans 5:2-4: *"And we boast in the hope of the glory of God. Not only so, but we also glory in our sufferings, because we know that suffering produces perseverance; perseverance, character; and character, hope."*

A great deal of Paul's suffering involved the inner anxiety and even anguish over the condition of the young Gentile churches for which he had been given the responsibility. Being in prison, Paul was forced to persevere because there was no way to take matters into his own hands, as I'm sure he would have liked. Perseverance molded his character and reaffirmed that without the power of God he could do absolutely nothing but pray and wait.

Most importantly, perseverance gave Paul time to contemplate his nothingness and grow in his trust in God. Once our identity-perspective is transformed into a perspective of nothingness, there is nothing left but hope. And hope is powerful — the product of a nothingness confidently rooted in the One from whom all real hope emerges. Paul might have been trapped physically in a prison cell under Roman authority, but with his thoughts on the power and promises of God he was enslaved to nobody.

It is impossible to grow in our gratitude for mountaintop living if mountaintop living is all we know. Contrast is important for balanced and secure spiritual living. We have to decide whether to live in a mountaintop ivory tower with a heart full of entitlement and ingratitude, or to trust the hard times to help produce the spiritual virtues necessary to being a disciple of Christ.

Humility enables us to see the unseen spiritual truths through the eyes of faith, at which time the valleys actually become the mountaintops. We are empowered after we enter the valley with a surrendered heart full of hope and gratitude for what we are going to learn. It is only in the valleys can we discover the power of a living hope as Peter describes it in 1 Peter 1:3: *"Praise be to the God and Father of our Lord Jesus Christ! In his great mercy he has given us new birth into a living hope through the resurrection of Jesus Christ from the dead."* For hope to be living it has to change our perspective and emotional response now when called to live sacrificially for others and to persevere through the direst of circumstances.

In God's kingdom resurrection has no meaning without death, humility will be illusive without suffering, and hope and faith will remain lifeless without trials. When we understand the importance of the relationship between suffering and spiritual transformation is when the valleys and the mountaintops begin to merge into one experience. The mountaintops flood the valleys with gratitude and faith, which fuel a living hope in all circumstances. Once it becomes difficult to distinguish between a valley and a mountaintop, we can be confident that we took the correct fork in the road in our journey to the nothingness of Christ.

Chapter Six

HUMILITY AND LEADERSHIP

Moreover, as you Philippians know, in the early days of your acquaintance with the gospel, when I set out from Macedonia, not one church shared with me in the matter of giving and receiving, except you only; for even when I was in Thessalonica, you sent me aid more than once when I was in need. Not that I desire your gifts; what I desire is that more be credited to your account. I have received full payment and have more than enough. I am amply supplied, now that I have received from Epaphroditus the gifts you sent. They are a fragrant offering, an acceptable sacrifice, pleasing to God. And my God will meet all your needs according to the riches of his glory in Christ Jesus. (PHILIPPIANS 4:15-19)

Serving as a leader in the in the full-time ministry, supported financially by the church, has many challenges to the on-going development of humility in a minister's life. Foundational to effective leadership is the humility or "nothingness" that Jesus demonstrated in his life, ministry, and teaching.

Yet, what is this humility supposed to look like in order to set the right example as a leader of God's people? We're called to be powerful soldiers of Christ, yet how do humility and powerful leadership work together in the same heart? Unfortunately,

Hollywood tends to depict "ministers" as soft-spoken and frail, always ready to give non-controversial, gentle, religious answers to life's challenges. Yet, how is this consistent with the ruggedness of say, John the Baptist, or the penetrating preaching of Jesus himself? How does someone find the balance between a Jesus who tenderly touched lepers with a Jesus who turned over the money changers' tables in the temple and drove them out with a whip? Those of us who lean temperamentally towards the "whipping" side of Jesus should seek the gentler side of Jesus as well. Those who are by nature gentle should realize that a spiritual "whip" can be a useful tool when wielded correctly.

The institutionalizing of the church, that is, the process involved in the development of a tightly-woven working leadership, is a serious challenge to every leadership. As the church grows and the leadership structure becomes more complex, how members are evaluated and the way church business is conducted can easily become a standard in itself.

If a church is to stay on-course biblically it is critical that leaders continue to lead according to God's intentions and not according to a leadership perspective and tradition as defined solely by the institution. Just as a God-defined leadership is critical to the health and fruit of the church, worldly leadership on the other hand, can devastate and destroy the church.

The Necessity of Leadership

So Christ himself gave the apostles, the prophets, the evangelists, the pastors and teachers to equip his people for works of service, so that the body of Christ may be built up until we all reach unity in the faith and in the knowledge of the Son of God and become mature, attaining to the whole measure of the fullness of Christ. (EPHESIANS 4:11-13)

Without question, if the church wants to be united, knowledgeable about Christ, and spiritually mature, qualified disciples need to take on the leadership ministries which are in line with their talents and applicable to the church today— elders, teachers, and evangelists.

The church should be appreciative and willing to support these ministers with our prayers and finances. Paul said in 1 THESSALONIANS 5:12-13; *"Now we ask you, brothers and sisters, to acknowledge those who work hard among you, who care for you in the Lord and who admonish you. Hold them in the highest regard in love because of their work. Live in peace with each other."*

Though this passage also involves Christians outside of full-time work, it certainly applies to the church staff. The admonishment is not to resist leadership but to be encouraging and thankful for their hard work.

The Minister and Church Support

As in Philippi, some in the church in Corinth had become critical of Paul, and for whatever reasons, were ashamedly not holding Paul *in the highest regard*, resistant to providing him financial support. In defense of his right to be supported Paul said the following. Though a somewhat lengthy quotation it is important to our discussion and I quote it here for the convenience of the reader. In particular, notice the solidity of Paul's argument.

> *This is my defense to those who sit in judgment on me. Don't we have the right to food and drink? Don't we have the right to take a believing wife along with us, as do the other apostles and the Lord's brothers and Cephas? Or is it only I and Barnabas who lack the right to not work for a living? Who serves as a soldier at his own expense? Who plants a vineyard and does not eat its*

grapes? . . . If we have sown spiritual seed among you, is it too much if we reap a material harvest from you? If others have this right of support from you, shouldn't we have it all the more? But we did not use this right. On the contrary, we put up with anything rather than hinder the gospel of Christ . . . In the same way, the Lord has commanded that those who preach the gospel should receive their living from the gospel.

But I have not used any of these rights. And I am not writing this in the hope that you will do such things for me, for I would rather die than allow anyone to deprive me of this boast. For when I preach the gospel, I cannot boast, since I am compelled to preach. Woe to me if I do not preach the gospel! If I preach voluntarily, I have a reward; if not voluntarily, I am simply discharging the trust committed to me. What then is my reward? Just this: that in preaching the gospel I may offer it free of charge, and so not make full use of my rights as a preacher of the gospel.
(1 CORINTHIANS 9:9-18)

Is it right to expect our ministers to work full-time in the secular world while bearing the responsibility for the spiritual well-being of the church? Obviously, God doesn't think so. Yet, in this particular situation, Paul relinquished his right for financial support and was willing to minister free of charge due to the critical attitudes within the Corinthian congregation.

Paul believed that preaching without support in the midst of the turmoil was best and was willing to become nothing for the sake of the overall well-being of the church. What is "right" is sometimes very wrong, and it takes a transformed identity-perspective as discussed above, as well as much wisdom and humility to distinguish between the two.

In order to get by, Paul became a tentmaker and worked alongside Aquila and Priscilla in the tent trade in Corinth. (ACTS 18:1-3) The Corinthian criticalness of Paul was tragic in light of the fact that Paul planted the church and continued to bear the burden for maturing the church, as well as other churches in the area.

We can only imagine how much more Paul could have done if he had full financial support and did not have to spend time making tents. However, what is important here to understand is that Paul's "doings" did not determine his "being"—his true identity. He considered himself a preacher of the Gospel regardless of his source of income.

It is normal to have the picture that Paul only tinkered in the tent trade for a few hours a week because of his busy ministry to the church. Yet, he supported himself full-time. I'm not sure what the pay scale was for tentmakers or how many days it took to make a tent, but with what I know about the trades in the first century I can only envision it being a meager living with long hours—no retirement, health or life insurance, financial security, or direct deposits. Nowhere close to a "secure" future as the world defines security.

However, while it is lamentable in one sense that Paul had to work as a tentmaker, God considered it an important part of his journey downward into the humility of Christ. Full-time ministers must always guard themselves against a **sense of entitlement**. God might well have another plan for their spiritual development.

A sense of entitlement has a way of squeezing out the proper gratitude we should have for what we do receive. Though ministers might have the right to financial support from a biblical perspective, to Paul, his rights were only part of the total equation.

When a church is small, many non-staff people by necessity need to be part of the decision-making process because of a limited number of staff. However, once a church begins to grow more staff is added and the need for the input of non-staff members lessens. If a leadership is not careful, all of the critical decisions for the church end up being made by full-time staff. This can create a bias in church decisions, and cause unrest among the more mature disciples.

It should be of particular concern when those making the major financial decisions for the church are supported full-time by the church. Anytime someone depends on a source of revenue for their material survival it is normal to want to decide where that revenue should be spent, and particularly to insure they personally are still included. The temptation is to overlook the real needs of the fellowship or what might be best for the church.

This is not to say that only full-time ministry leaders face these challenges. Every disciple in the business world faces the daily temptation to compromise principle in order to get close to the right people to get ahead. Ministers and their families are uniquely challenged in this regard and need our encouragement all the more.

Though often unfairly expected to be the most humble, wise, or spiritual in a congregation the minister is perceived as the "leader" in all church settings. He or she is under constant pressure to be "somebody" at the center of things. To be on call 24/7 and expected to have the answers to the all of the members' problems, even those regarding financial and business matters.

Yet, some ministers have never worked in the business world where the majority of their members spend their lives. Young ministers often finish their university work and go straight into the full-time ministry. With no practical experience involving what their members live through, preaching and teaching can lack important insight, understanding, relevancy, and practical and reasonable application.

Jesus did not begin his ministry until he was 30 years old. Up to that time he worked as a carpenter, robed as a peasant's son, yet growing in his understanding of the struggles of those around him. The more experiences we encounter, in and out of the ministry, the more far-reaching our influence will be. If Jesus did not begin his ministry until he was 30, perhaps some time in the working world would do all ministers some good.

From my experience, I suggest that ministers separate themselves as far as possible from the financial matters in the church. Too much involvement can raise suspicions about motives and self-interest, and can even lead to the enslaving sins associated with materialism and greed. The ministry staff should be careful not to be in a position to have the final word on church expenditures for that very reason.

Though money was obviously a concern to Paul, it appears never to have affected his passion, commitment, integrity, where he ministered, or most importantly, his insight into what was best. His love for people was the driving passion in his life. Financial support was only part of fulfilling that passion. His passion to follow Christ into his suffering is what freed him from an unhealthy dependence on position, authority, or support to carry out his ministry.

Paul's love for people and ministry would have made the present distinction in the church between being "in the ministry" and not being in the ministry unknown to Paul. Support never affected Paul's sense of mission or role. His identity-perspective was unaffected by full support, partial support, or no support at all. He was "in the ministry" regardless and he never withdrew from his responsibilities or commitment to Christ.

That is why he was able to say, *"I know what it is to be in need, and I know what it is to have plenty. I have learned the secret of being content in any and every situation, whether well fed or hungry, whether living in plenty or in want. I can do all this through him who gives me strength."* (PHILIPPIANS 4:12-13)

The key phrase here is, "through him." In the context of Philippians this is not a mystical emotional experience, but involves a deep reliance on God's power in order to turn from the world and follow a cross-driven Messiah. Contentment in "any and every situation" must have a supernatural source of power. Why is this contentment a secret? Because the secret is unlocked only for those far down the road to nothingness, who have been able to loosen the shackles of a dependence on material things for contentment.

Having served in the ministry for nearly three decades I can say with confidence that most ministers face the ever-present tension between the radical preaching and lifestyle of Christ and the early church, and the inevitable threat that lifestyle brings to their financial, institutional, and personal security.

Unless ministers have an identity-perspective deeply centered in Christ, the "happiness" of the people too often becomes the primary hermeneutical influence on the preaching and teaching of the leaders. Church becomes more about theatrics, entertainment, and making people feel good.

Giving the listeners what they want to hear certainly guarantees a more secure future for a church staff, at least in this life. Paul taught the following in 2 TIMOTHY 4:3-4; *"For the time will come when people will not put up with sound doctrine. Instead, to suit their own desires, they will gather around them a great number of teachers to say what their itching ears want to hear. They will turn their ears away from the truth and turn aside to myths."*

In other words, the mark of a false teacher is someone whose prime motive is to keep people happy—to give them ". . . *what their itching ears want to hear.*" For example, financial "Prosperity Theology" teaches that the more money you give to the "God," the more God will bless you financially. Parts of the Bible are twisted, overlooked, and ignored. The standard becomes not what God wants, but what the people want. Preachers of this persuasion serve a theological buffet and always seem to have what everybody wants.

This theology ignores, however, that Philippians was written from a prison cell, Jesus died in poverty on a cross, and John the Baptist lived in the desert, ate locusts, and was beheaded. These men were not exactly in the people-pleasing business. Financial prosperity was nowhere on their radar.

Because of the insecurity of losing a position, the preaching style of career ministers has a tendency to change over the years. Radical preaching and teaching usually defines young ministers—men and women with a great vision, and lots of energy, exactly what institutional and traditional churches need.

Yet, as the years go on and ministers reach middle age, they are often trapped by life's circumstances and worries in what I refer to as the "Great Middle Age Compromise." The idea of "going along to get along"—avoiding conflict, no rocking the boat, gracious preaching, shaking hands with a big smile at the back door, and everybody goes home happy. Not everybody went home happy after Paul arrived in Corinth. And it certainly wasn't the "happy" people who crucified Jesus.

Granted, preaching needs to evolve as we spiritually mature, but it should never compromise the radical message of Christ and the lifestyle it demands. In fact, spiritual maturity involves deepening in our convictions about defending the truth.

Ministers should not allow money, position, or prestige determine their degree of commitment to the particular church in which they serve. When higher paid positions or more long term secure opportunities become available in other churches, the temptation is to move because of the growing need for more support or to have a wider political influence.

What would cause a minister to leave the flock that God has entrusted to him? If we believe that we are called to full-time church work and "anointed" so to speak over the ministry, then what changed the calling?

It could very well be that God will call us to a place with greater resources and opportunities to more fully develop our God-given talents to have a greater range of influence for his cause. But to move primarily because of a bigger paycheck or to stay on the payroll shows a concerning disconnect between a shepherd and his flock.

Why did Paul continue to minister to churches critical of him and unwilling to support him? Most ministers would find it very difficult to continue to serve in those circumstances. It would be a sign from God to move on. And sure, there are legitimate reasons for a minister to move, but if his identity-perspective is not intact, he can easily confuse for the will of God his desire for advancement, more support, or to avoid conflict.

If someone is looking for a "career" or regards the ministry as a career, it's better to go into the business or corporate world where careers are made. If the ministry becomes a career more than a calling it is very difficult to completely embrace and preach the truth. The ministry is not a business or a "career" path but a life devoted to meeting the needs of the disciples, sometimes with support and sometimes without. It's a way of life and not just a way to pay for life.

The passage cited at the beginning of this chapter provides great insight into Paul's heart and identity-perspective. It is obvious that Paul's support was a constant issue. At that particular time no other churches had committed to Paul's support except for the church in Philippi. Yet, nowhere, do we see Paul demanding payment or using his apostolic authority to coerce the other churches to give. Because of his indulgence in the nothingness of Christ, he was able to be grateful, content, and to have a deeper dependence on God in the midst of his financial and political realities.

Unity in the Church

Therefore if you have any encouragement from being united with Christ, if any comfort from his love, if any common sharing in the Spirit, if any tenderness and compassion, then make my joy complete by being like-minded, having the same love, being one in spirit and of one mind. Do nothing out of selfish ambition or vain conceit. Rather, in humility value others above yourselves, not looking to your own interests but each of you to the interests of the others. (PHILIPPIANS 2:1-4)

Every minister will have to deal with disunity, relationship dysfunction, and critical people in the congregation from time to time. It is inevitable and therefore, should be one of those "accepted expectations" we discussed. The important lesson here involves how to apply the humility of Christ to deal with criticalness and disunity in the church.

With so many options involving churches to attend, church staff can be tempted to either give the critical members what they want, or stand their ground with a take-it-or-leave-it attitude. It's always easier to maintain control if all of the "negative" people leave. This attitude is sadly too common among church staffs, yet so far from the thinking of Paul.

Paul viewed his troubled churches through the windows of God's love, patience, and grace. Notice how he begins his letter to the Corinthian church which was also a disunified church with many internal problems, both doctrinal and practical:

> To the church of God in Corinth, to those sanctified in Christ Jesus and called to be his holy people, together with all those everywhere who call on the name of our Lord Jesus Christ — their Lord and ours: Grace and peace to you from God our Father and the Lord Jesus Christ. I always thank my God for you because of his grace given you in Christ Jesus. For in him you have been enriched in every way — with all kinds of speech and with all knowledge — God thus confirming our testimony about Christ among you. Therefore you do not lack any spiritual gift as you eagerly wait for our Lord Jesus Christ to be revealed. He will also keep you firm to the end, so that you will be blameless on the day of our Lord Jesus Christ. God is faithful, who has called you into fellowship with his Son, Jesus Christ our Lord.
> (1 CORINTHIANS 1:2-9)

Without reading the rest of the letter, one would think that Paul is writing to a very spiritually mature congregation, yet in light of all the problems in the church, this passage appears to be full of flattery and over-exaggerated praise. Or, we have a valuable lesson to learn.

What I believe we have here is the example of someone who could "see through" and beyond the problems to focus on the true identity of the church, which was a fellowship of believers sanctified in Christ, possessors of the grace of God, and *"enriched in every way."* Sure there were issues to be resolved, but with the proper perspective of the Church's identity in mind, Paul was able to navigate the troubled waters. The church was valuable and worthy of whatever sacrifices Paul needed to make. After all, Jesus died for her.

When we believe in someone's identity as one of God's special children, and consider their interests more important than ours, we will be better listeners and more sympathetic, patient, and helpful. All Christians are "God-placed" in the body of Christ. Ministers' perspectives of their members, even critical and "needy" members, must include these realities.

Jesus showed us the importance of "seeing through," beyond the external problems and physical limitations of people, into the heart and value of each individual soul. His ministry to the "unclean," disabled, rejected, and cursed leaves us an example of what our perspectives as ministers should be. Ministers have been called to minister to everyone, not just the leaders and the multi-talented members. Jesus summed up his ministry in this way; *"It is not the healthy who need a doctor, but the sick. I have not come to call the righteous, but sinners."* (MARK 2:17)

Our Need for One Another

One of the greatest challenges of the full-time minister is to keep a balanced schedule between time with family, ministry staff, and the rest of the church. The higher up one advances in ministerial responsibilities more time is usually devoted to leaders and ministry staff—the more mature members of the church.

It is important to remember Paul's analogy between the physical body and the church; *"And the head cannot say to the feet, 'I don't need you'"* (1 CORINTHIANS 12:21). In actuality the physical head of the body can do much better without the feet than the feet can do without the head, that is, if we view the body only in terms of its physicality. But if we apply the illustration of the physical body to the function of the body of Christ as Paul did, the relational dynamics are completely different.

The truth is, both the head and the feet are needed by the other. Leadership in the world is hierarchal by nature with an emphasis on the vertical positional aspects of relationships. But the church is not a karate class with various belt colors determining the positional status of the participants.

Rather, in the church the horizontal dynamics of human relationships—the one-on-one, adult-to-adult relationships— must also be cultivated and emphasized, alongside with the necessary leadership structure. Paul wrote; *"those parts of the body that seem to be weaker are indispensable,"* (1 CORINTHIANS 12:22). This is so contrary to how we normally think. How can the weaker members of the church be indispensable? Aren't the strong members the ones who survive, are dependable, give the most, and basically hold the church together? Aren't the weak the main source of the church's problems, who drain the energy from the strong? Wouldn't it be better if the church was comprised only of highly driven members with strong personalities in order to take the message to the world?

The word, *seem*, is critical to this passage, *those parts of the body that **seem** to be weaker.* Just as with many principles which Jesus taught, what appears or seems one way to the world is the opposite in God's mind— *"the last will be first, and the first will be last"* (MATTHEW 20:17); *"whoever takes the lowly position of this child is the greatest in the kingdom of heaven"* (MATTHEW 18:4); and *"what people value highly is detestable in God's sight"* (LUKE 16:15).

The journeys of the "weak" are often the most iconic, most respected and commended by the Lord because of the consistent spiritual wilderness experiences they have had to endure. During the ministry of Christ the list is quite lengthy—the Canaanite woman (MATTHEW 15), sinful woman (LUKE 7), centurion (MATTHEW 8), blind man (JOHN 9), Samaritan woman (JOHN 4), the child (MATTHEW 18:4), as well as fishermen, tax-collectors, and peasants.

There is a big difference between the experience of a disciple who rises early Sunday morning in the sweltering heat of a poverty-stricken country to work for a few hours before walking several miles to church and then home again only to work for the rest of the day; and the experiences of someone who reluctantly climbs into an air-conditioned car to drive to a comfortable temperature-controlled church building, afterwards to enjoy a big Sunday lunch and settle in for a nice long nap. Who might appear the spiritually stronger "successful" type in this comparison is obviously the weaker and the weaker the stronger.

Position, Authority, and the Ministry

Keep watch over yourselves and all the flock of which the Holy Spirit has made you overseers. Be shepherds of the church of God, which he bought with his own blood. I know that after I leave, savage wolves will come in among you and will not spare the flock. Even from your own number men will arise and distort the truth in order to draw away disciples after them. So be on your guard! Remember that for three years I never stopped warning each of you night and day with tears. (ACTS 20:28-31)

This admonition cannot be taken lightly. "Savage wolves" are described as those who distort the truth and do not spare the flock by persuading disciples to follow them. In serious church disputes it is important to determine exactly who the wolves are.

In order for this to be accomplished it is important to discern between constructive and destructive criticism. It is detrimental to the unity of the church when ministers' insecurities overwhelm them to the point that they become suspicious of all criticism, that somehow "input" is a sign of a potential "savage wolf." No doubt unresolved criticalness can quickly lead to disunity and factions within the fellowship, however, constructive input is valuable and every leader should seriously consider it.

Whoever appears critical initially, when listened and ministered to with humility and concern, might well become a life-long friend and loyal supporter. Every minister has to make sure **he** does not become the problem by resisting true constructive input and thus hurting the flock, while persuading others to continue to follow him despite his resistance to the truth.

Leaders should never judge another brother or sister as not doing well spiritually, or as being divisive, based on different perspectives and opinions. "Divisive" is an accusation that should be seldom used initially in any relationship dysfunction.

How people voice their perspective may become an issue of divisiveness, but the perspective itself should always be respected and considered, even if only initially.

One of the greatest pieces of advice for relationship dysfunction is found in the book of James: *"My dear brothers and sisters, take note of this: Everyone should be quick to listen, slow to speak and slow to become angry, because human anger does not produce the righteousness that God desires"* (James 1:19-20).

Ministers are the ones who most often deal with critical and "difficult" people. It is easy to get worn down and to feel defensive for the ministry and for the church. Even before a difficult counseling session begins with two opposing parties, usually lots of talking has taken place on both sides and everyone enters their bunkers with their helmets on.

Everyone has a need to be heard, which involves more than an hour appointment. It takes time to give a real hearing to a person's life story. What have been his or her life shaping experiences? Who have been most influential in their lives? What events have taught them the most about God and life in general? Getting to know people personally is foundational to relationship and disunity resolution.

Listening is a spiritual art form and ministers need to learn as much as they can about it. It disarms a critical attitude when we sincerely listen with a determination to understand. It empowers those being heard and strengthens a person's identity-perspective regarding the value he or she brings to the body of Christ. It also opens a clearer window into the heart and motives and provides a greater possibility of reaching some level of meaningful resolution.

Proper and helpful communication in relationships is not learned overnight. Many people have the greatest of intentions but lack the skill to communicate those intentions in a constructive way. Every minister is called to prepare the church for works of service, and learning to communicate with others as we work and serve together should be a pivotal part of that training.

The membership should never feel they have to cross an obstacle course in order to be heard and have their perspective considered. Talented people want to have their talents utilized for God, and if they are not given a vision and an environment in which to develop their spiritual skills, they will more than likely move on to a healthier fellowship of disciples, or stagnate spiritually.

Paul said, *"Finally, brothers and sisters, whatever is true, whatever is noble, whatever is right, whatever is pure, whatever is lovely, whatever is admirable—if anything is excellent or praiseworthy—think about such things"* (PHILIPPIANS 4:8).

Paul's admonishment is immensely practical when dealing with the "opposition." If we would only start any attempt at reconciliation with these virtues in mind the outcome will always be more positive. The connection between disciples needs to be the passion to see what is true, noble, right, pure, lovely, and admirable in one another, and not what is suspicious, legalistically judgmental, and distrustful. We should concentrate on the good in one another before we turn to the issues that might divide us.

Love of Position

With the constant pressure to be "somebody" in our world it is very difficult to stay on the road to nothingness. It is easier to make decisions and keep people at a distance through an emphasis on authority and position. Yet, the ultimate challenge is to trust that if we continue downward in humility and self-denial others will trust that we are God-led leaders and will want to follow.

I encourage every minister to strive for honesty with themselves about enjoying the limelight and having a strong influence over the thinking of people. It's a normal struggle. But the power of God is not found in the limelight or on pedestals, but in weakness and the recognition of our nothingness before God.

Besides, the real pedestal is at the right hand of God which all disciples occupy. Paul said, *"And God raised us up with Christ and seated us with him in the heavenly realms in Christ Jesus"* (EPHESIANS 2:6) If being seated with Christ in the heavenly realms is not good enough to ease our drive for "somethingness," God has nothing else to offer.

A leader cannot prevent people from looking up to him, but he can prevent himself from becoming a legend in his or her own mind. No matter how people view us, whether they look up to or down on us, our true identity-perspective must stay rooted in a suffering Messiah whose prime objective was not the affirmation of the self, but rather, it's denial. It is only because of what he became — nothing — that we are anything. We are simply his instruments.

Jesus emphasized the importance of this understanding when he said, *"Blessed are the poor in spirit, for theirs is the kingdom of heaven."* (MATTHEW 5:3) Not poor financially necessarily, but poor in spirit, an essential aspect of the journey to nothingness. Decisions in the church cannot be about who is right as when entitlement and position are prominent, but about what is right, as when Jesus gave up his right to life and Paul his right to financial support.

If ministers cannot find contentment in their humble state before God and others, then their identity-perspective can be detrimental to the growth and unity of the church. Because of insecurity, any mentoring of future church leaders will be self-serving and a quenching of the talent and movement of the Spirit in their lives.

A minister's humility before God is critical or ministers are in danger of creating an environment in which those they are spiritually mentoring become dependent on the minister's perspectives and methodologies, rather than learning to develop their own convictions. It's important to remember that any Christian put under a minister's care is first and foremost a disciple of Christ.

Ministers must be careful not to select staff based merely on the basis of friendship, personality, or appearance, but more importantly on the bases of depth of spirituality, knowledge of God's word, and commitment to Christ. Sometimes unity of the staff is so emphasized that anyone with another perspective is viewed as critical or "not on board." With imperfect people mentoring or discipling can never be a one-way dynamic.

Questions over who is the most talented in the church can be haunting to ministers and make church staffs insecure. Without humility, a high skill-set in a member can make a minister insecure—an insecurity which if not checked will lead to favoritism and elitism. Church leaders with an ailing identity-perspective feel more comfortable surrounded by loyal and supportive members.

In other words, ministers must be careful not to compete with or be intimidated by members of their congregation. Rather, it should be the goal to help every member develop their talents to the full for God, even if those gifts exceed the talents of the minister himself.

A football coach never expects to compete at the same level with his players, but his hope is that every player will go far beyond what he could have ever achieved himself. His pride and purpose is in pouring himself into the development of others. He, in essence, must become nothing in order for others to become something. Favoritism in the church always leaves some of the most spiritual talent on the bench. A minister's primary role is to train. Though a football coach should never expect to throw a football with the same power and accuracy as his quarterback, he will still find satisfaction in the fact that his coaching contributed to his quarterback overall success.

I realize that every situation has a host of variables to consider. The answers regarding the many questions involving one's role in the church and what is best are seldom black and white. Yet, what is critical to realize, as with our human bodies, is all the members of the body of Christ have dependent and overlapping relationships with each other.

There are important insights concerning this idea in Paul's words to the Corinthians. *"Just as a body, though one, has many parts, but all its many parts form one body, so it is with Christ. For we were all baptized by one Spirit so as to form one body—whether Jews or Gentiles, slave or free—and we were all given the one Spirit to drink. Even so the body is not made up of one part but of many"* (1 CORINTHIANS 12:12-14).

Leaders with a twisted identity-perspective view themselves as the "eye," one of the most prized parts of the physical body. The problem is not in being the eye. The eye does set the direction for the whole body as the minister sets the direction for the church. The problem is how the eye views the other parts of the body.

Jesus said, *"The eye is the lamp of the body. If your eyes are healthy, your whole body will be full of light. But if your eyes are unhealthy, your whole body will be full of darkness. If then the light within you is darkness, how great is that darkness!"* (MATTHEW 6:22-23)

In this context, Jesus draws a parallel between the eye of the physical body and spiritual perspective. If we view life from a perspective of nothingness then we can be confident that our journey is headed in the right direction—that our spiritual eyes are clear.

On the other hand, if our spiritual perspective, particularly our identity-perspective, is distorted with the need for respect, prominence, power, and money, then our existence is in the darkness. And if darkness is what is leading us, then the power of darkness multiplies in our lives and the lives of others.

The principle here has obvious application for leadership roles. If a minister's "eye" or overall perspective of himself is not centered on Christ, but distorted by insecurity and the need for power and authority, the result will be a competitive and authority-driven fellowship.

The minister in this case is most comfortable only in relationships where he is the adult and everyone else is the child. An unhealthy dependence is developed and the members with different opinions, or who have the preaching and teaching talent to compete with the minister, are kept at a distance and in their place. In other words, the eye is saying to the rest of body, "I don't need you."

A mature and wise leader recognizes the importance of his or her role, while at the same time recognizing the value and importance of the other parts of the body. A famous professional football quarterback might get the entire spotlight, but deep down in his heart, he knows without his team working alongside of him he has no chance of winning. Whatever "fame" he might have is because he is standing on the shoulders of other people.

The makings of a healthy congregation demand mutual adult-to-adult relationships which lead to an understanding that everyone in the body of Christ might have different roles, but they all wear the same uniform. Every Christian needs to be on the field of play. No one sits on the bench in the kingdom of God— *"we were all given the one Spirit to drink"* (1 CORINTHIANS 12:13).

Jesus faced a positional challenge in his ministry. When the crowds wanted to make him a political king after he miraculously fed the 5,000. He responded to the offer by leaving the area (JOHN 6:14-15). The fact that he left is important. The last thing Jesus needed was to feel that he had become "something" on his journey to being nothing—that he somehow needed a political kingdom in order to be successful. He was already the King of Kings and the empowering nothingness he embraced enabled him to navigate and overcome the haunting doubts in his humanity regarding his identity and self-worth.

The challenge for ministers is the fear of leaving an area where prominence is possible. Prominence has an appealing, almost irresistible attraction because of the respect and consequent financial security it provides. But we must ask ourselves; security in what? How others feel about us? That we will most likely always have a job? Is our main purpose to ensure our future financial security or to live day to day completely immersed in the now and the nothingness of Christ as Paul was for the sake of the Gospel?

Ministers must allow their motives to be tested and refined regarding not only why they entered the ministry but why they remain in the ministry. There is within all of us a deep fear of the wildernesses experiences, one of which is being without a position and unemployed, yet these experiences are a vital part of staying on the road to complete nothingness. We must be willing to give up a position or to even leave the "ministry" if they become an obstacle to a deeper understanding of the nothingness of Christ or to the betterment of the church.

Entering the ministry should be the beginning of a **descent** into the nothingness of Christ—into his humility, love, and sacrificial living. But for some it is an **ascent** into a world much like the corporate world—a world of position, influence, respect, and authority. Jesus began his ministry by going down into the wilderness and fasting for 40 days. Ministers often enter their ministries by taking the road up to the mountaintop.

Regarding Christ's own experience, Paul wrote; *"What does "he ascended" mean except that he also descended to the lower, earthly regions? He who descended is the very one who ascended higher than all the heavens, in order to fill the whole universe"* (EPHESIANS 4:9-10).

Descension always precedes **ascension** in the kingdom of God. We confuse the two and want to put the cart before the horse. As we discussed above, at the beginning of his ministry while Jesus was fasting in the wilderness Satan offered him all the kingdoms of the world if he would just bow down and worship him. (MATTHEW 4:8-9) Satan was tempting Jesus to initiate an ascension into a world of entitlement and splendor and to take his focus off of his descensional commitments.

Notice again the example of Jesus:

And being found in appearance as a man, he humbled himself by becoming obedient to death—even death on a cross! Therefore

God exalted him to the highest place and gave him the name that is above every name . . . (PHILIPPIANS 2:8-9)

And now notice once again the promise that God has given us:

But because of his great love for us, God, who is rich in mercy, made us alive with Christ even when we were dead in transgressions—it is by grace you have been saved. And God raised us up with Christ and seated us with him in the heavenly realms in Christ Jesus, in order that in the coming ages he might show the incomparable riches of his grace, expressed in his kindness to us in Christ Jesus. (EPHESIAN 2:4-7)

If we commit to a life of descension God will take care of our ascension. God has made abundantly clear that our resurrection and ascension are his business and descension is ours. And God always takes care of his business. The question is; will we take care of ours?

After leaving the ministry I distinctly remember sitting on the side of the bed one morning with a deep dread of what the future held for me. No more positions, financial security, influence, travel experiences, speaking engagements, phone calls, prominence, and respect to hold me up. I was the low man on the totem pole. My descension had begun.

The most revealing part of my journey was that I never realized until I left the ministry how confused my identity-perspective had become and how dependent I was on position and respect as a full-time minister. Yet, it is the "going without" that molds our identity-perspectives and is the challenge that refines our faith.

My first job after leaving the ministry involved the selling of medical machines. At the age of fifty, all the experience I had was ministry related. I had worked for a time while in my graduate studies as an iron worker but that provided little help in selling medical machines.

The first obstacle I encountered was the pain of rejection. After living off of the admiration and respect of others for most of my life, this was a hard reality to embrace. And it was an everyday experience. I was a salesman pure and simple, and for the most part, nobody likes a salesman. Even though the machines I represented could bring a great deal of healing and revenue into the doctor's office, the time and energy it took to convince a doctor of a machine's potential was agonizing.

After some years of medical machine sells, I switched to the field of life insurance. Though I had grown in my ability to withstand rejection to some extent, life insurance sales is also a marathon in enduring rejection, though I felt a greater sense of satisfaction helping people plan for their financial futures.

When initially experiencing the rejection, I was far from a healthy identity-perspective. That's why it hurt so much. I felt insulted, disrespected, rejected, and sometimes hated. It has taken some years to recognize how valuable those experiences were to a better understanding of the humility of Christ.

I was just selling machines and found it difficult to separate how people viewed the machine with how they viewed me. Somehow I had let a medical machine become part of my identity-perspective. The physical has a way of infiltrating and influencing our view of ourselves.

I leased an expensive car and bought expensive suits to "impress" my potential clients. That car and those clothes also became part of my perspective of myself. I often thought that if I could just get a doctor to ride in my BMW, then he would be so impressed with me that he would buy a machine. My hopes for success were in my material possessions.

I realize that any successful business man must consider issues of image and the importance of making a good first impression. I'm not promoting wearing ragged suits and driving rusty cars as some sort of spiritual sales strategy, but I am suggesting we all take a hard look into why we own what we do and what is the source of our confidence.

Jesus Christ did not come to sell product, but to give his life and offer us life. He faced the same obstacles that we all face—scorn, rejection and disrespect. However, because he came to become nothing, the issues that we feel are monumental were but minor inconveniences to a man whose identity-perspective was intact and on a clear course.

Authority

With the role of minister, like any other leadership role, comes some level of authority. In the book of Hebrews it teaches: *"Obey your leaders and submit to them. They keep watch over your souls as men who much give an account"* (HEBREWS 13:17). Though the Greek text does not include the word *authority*, the use of *obey* and *submit* imply the reality of authority which is why some translations include it.

Another important passage which involves the authority of a minister is found in Paul's letter to Titus: *"Teach these things. Encourage and rebuke with all authority. Do not let anyone despise you"* (TITUS 2:15).

This passage does include a Greek word for *authority* which should put to rest the question whether the minister has some authority in the church.

In both of the texts quoted above, a minister's authority is limited to the spiritual well-being of the church. The writer to the Hebrews states that leaders keep watch over our souls—those things involving our spiritual lives. Paul does admonish Titus to encourage and rebuke with all authority, but only as it pertains to *these things*—the contents of TITUS 2:1-4—and their practical application. Other areas of life are left to opinion and personal conscience.

The challenge for every minister involves how the humility of Jesus should be applied to the wielding of authority. For an "authoritative" position to fit within the theological framework of the nothingness of Christ it must involve a consistent "washing of the feet" of the disciples and living sacrificially for them. Authority wielded from any other platform will prove fatal to the hopes of a true, safe, and loving fellowship of God's people.

When a dispute arose among the disciples regarding who should sit at the right and left of Jesus in his kingdom, Jesus said; *"You know that the rulers of the Gentiles lord it over them, and their high officials exercise authority over them. Not so with you. Instead, whoever wants to become great among you must be your servant, and whoever wants to be first must be your slave— just as the Son of Man did not come to be served, but to serve, and to give his life as a ransom for many"* (MATTHEW 20: 25-28).

God-given authority in the church is to be completely upside down from how the world uses authority. God expects leadership to keep order and promote unity but not to be in the business of "ordering" others around. Authority in the church is rooted in example. A ministry position carries authority only if the minister is willing to set the example for what he is challenging his members to be. People do not generally follow a hypocrite.

The Minister and Confession

Therefore I will boast all the more gladly about my weaknesses, so that Christ's power may rest on me. That is why, for Christ's sake, I delight in weaknesses, in insults, in hardships, in persecutions, in difficulties. For when I am weak, then I am strong. (2 CORINTHIANS 12:9-10)

With the church's expectation that ministers are to be the most spiritual and capable of avoiding the problems the members struggle with, very few ministers boast about their weaknesses. Spiritual living, however, involves not only avoiding certain sins, but also knowing how to repent and overcome sin.

We generally do not want to acknowledge that our minister is also a sinner. Not a "real" sinner anyways. However, in order to set a more complete example, ministers need to be an example of openness and humility concerning their weaknesses.

One of the great hypocrisies ministers fall into is the one-way confession trap. We all struggle with concerns about image, but ministers have a greater burden in this regard because their role is to lead the church spiritually, and because spirituality is not an occupation but a way of life, they are always put to some extent on the "pedestal" by their members.

In the corporate world you put in your eight hours and go home; no one cares what you do after that, what your family is like, or what kind of marriage you have. You're going to receive a pay check regardless. You can have the worst personal life imaginable and all you have to do is put on some clean clothes, a friendly confident image, and show up at work. At the end of the day you can return to any kind of lifestyle you want.

Ministers, on the other hand, are always under the microscope. They are expected to set the example of righteousness, lead the prayer, say things in an appropriate professional manner, answer all the Bible questions, and have the perfect family.

Because of this, ministers are not inclined to confess their sins to the members of the church because it might tarnish what people think. Their image could be shattered. Even though ministers themselves resist and even hate the image, they nonetheless make part of their living from it.

The unrealistic assumptions we have involving the behavior of our ministers can lead them down a river channeled by other people's expectations, rather than by the Holy Spirit and personal conscience. The emphasis on image, whether from external sources or internal pride and insecurity, discourages ministers to throw themselves into the mix with the rest of the fellowship where confession, forgiveness, and mercy are bonding others members together. In order to confess and deal with their sins of lust, greed, self-righteousness, and other sins, ministers sometimes find themselves maintaining a secret code of silence--confessing only to people in higher level church positions and showing more mercy to other ministers than "regular" members.

If we are supposed to *delight in weaknesses* as Paul did (2 CORINTHIANS 12:10), then ministers must quiet the social and political factors which influence and hinder them from living open and confident lives. Many of the problems we hear ministers having such as adulterous affairs or financial mishandlings could have been avoided if they had been given or had taken the opportunity early in their ministries for consistent confession, honesty, brokenness, and repentance.

Confession needs to be a mutual exchange. Genuine confession from a heart of godly sorrow allows us to take one step further into the nothingness of Christ. This does not mean all sins confessed have to be public. The Bible does not tell us how many people we have to confess to for it to be legitimate. It just needs to happen. No booths or curtains to hide behind, just an honest walk into the light with another brother or sister, whether with a young disciple or someone who has been following Christ for years.

Ministers need to realize that they have "addiction" issues like everybody else. Not necessarily alcohol or drug-related, but dependencies regarding the need for respect, admiration, financial security, and prominence. These desires are just as dangerous to our identity-perspective as any drug we might put in our body. Every minister needs to treat these desires with the same seriousness that a sober alcoholic has to deal with his alcohol use, which is a daily openness regarding associated feelings and desires.

Most understand the importance of attending regular meetings with an individual or a group for support and the opportunity to be open—meetings in which title, education, wealth, position, and age are all left at the door. Ministers lead most of the meetings they attend so to be in a meeting not as someone with all of the answers, but someone who needs the answers, is a change in role and will require a radical transformation of one's identity-perspective.

We all have to view ourselves as "needy." A very refreshing experience is to feel the power of just being nothing, giving up the image, control, need for respect, and whatever else we're dependent on for our security. The closet needs to be opened and the skeletons released. We all need time in our lives when we can get out from behind the "political" images and feel the power of complete disclosure, surrender, and walking in the light—in other words, true spiritual living.

There is much contentment to be experienced with the understanding of what Paul meant when he said he delighted in weaknesses, insults, hardships, persecutions, and difficulties. What is an insult to someone with an identity-perspective filled with "nothingness?" What is there to insult if nothing is there? It should not matter if some critical members find out about a particular struggle we are going through or something in our past of which we are ashamed. An insult does nothing to change our true objective identity before God; it only has the potential of damaging our view of ourselves.

It is during persecutions and hardships when grace has its effect. The more we understand that the grace of God has brought us to the spiritual state of "somethingness"—our new identity as a forgiven child of God—the more we can rejoice at whatever the world throws at us. The world has nothing to intimidate someone who realizes his "nothingness" in this world and his "somethingness" in Christ.

The Minister and Education

The importance of education involving a growing understanding of the Word of God, whether formal or informal, cannot be overstated. If we have been called to follow the truth, then we are responsible to determine what that truth is. And that takes serious study, prayer, contemplation, humility, and hard work.

Because of the teaching responsibilities associated with the ministry, ministers have the added task of teaching the truths contained in the Bible. Paul told Timothy: *"As I urged you when I went into Macedonia, stay there in Ephesus so that you may command certain people not to teach false doctrines any longer or to devote themselves to myths and endless genealogies"* (1 TIMOTHY 4:3-4).

In order to command people not to teach false doctrines, we must first know what the true doctrines are—what the Bible actually teaches as opposed to opinion and biased interpretation. The application of the humility of Christ has huge implications for anyone desiring to know the truth. Jesus' words, *"Whoever wants to be my disciple must deny themselves,"* have no greater significance than in the area of determining what is true.

"Education" is a dangerous enterprise for any disciple in light of the academic environments of the world's educational institutions, particularly state colleges and universities. Those departments having to do with the origin, purpose, and destiny of Humankind are atheistic or agnostic regarding the existence of God.

The danger of education also involves the effect it can have on our identity-perspective. To someone determined to apply the humility of Christ to their spiritual lives, theological education is a legitimate opportunity to gain the tools to help build the kingdom of God. However, education often results in hearts full of arrogance, pride, and title and position-dependence. Look what happened to the Apostle Paul before he became a Christian. When pride goes unchecked the interpreter's conclusions most often will be irrational and miss the mark of sound interpretation. Paul said *"knowledge puffs up while love builds up"* (1 CORINTHIANS 8:1).

Paul also provides some useful insight when he says:

For the message of the cross is foolishness to those who are perishing, but to us who are being saved it is the power of God. For it is written:

*"I will destroy the wisdom of the wise;
the intelligence of the intelligent I will frustrate."*

Where is the wise person? Where is the teacher of the law? Where is the philosopher of this age? Has not God made foolish the wisdom of the world? For since in the wisdom of God the world through its wisdom did not know him, God was pleased through the foolishness of what was preached to save those who believe. Jews demand signs and Greeks look for wisdom, but we preach Christ crucified: a stumbling block to Jews and foolishness to Gentiles, but to those whom God has called, both Jews and Greeks, Christ the power of God and the wisdom of God. For the foolishness of God is wiser than human wisdom, and the weakness of God is stronger than human strength. (1 CORINTHIANS 1:18-25)

There are some word-plays important to this context. The quotation from Isaiah 29:14 seems to contain a contradiction in ideas. Why would God destroy the wisdom of the wise if wisdom is crucial to the application of God's Word, and if intelligence is so important to knowing God, why frustrate it?

God is not frustrating the legitimate use of intelligence or the proper use of wisdom, but rather, the thinking process of obstinate people who claim to be intelligent and wise, yet who in reality represent "intelligence" and "wisdom" gone seriously awry. Potential hampered by pride and self-concern.

When something is given to us, as is our intelligence, there is no basis to boast. How can we be prideful about the creation and existence of something we had nothing to do with? It is clear that we are not self-created. "Intelligent" people who never acknowledge the origin of what they have will never use their intelligence properly—like giving someone a boat who tries to drive it on the street.

A legitimate quest for education can quickly evolve into a self-serving quest for title and prestige. Degrees in biblical, theological, or philosophical studies can be very useful to the preaching, teaching, and defending of the Gospel, but can also lead one to pursue degrees as a measure of one's credibility and sense of self-worth. And for a title-dependent minister, not only is the degree itself important, but the prestige associated with various universities carries extra notoriety and prominence as well. As Solomon pointed out, there is always wind to chase (ECCLESIASTES 1:14).

The contribution to a more accurate understanding of the message of the Bible, both in academic institutions and in the church is a worthy live-long endeavor. Whatever knowledge is attained though should be for the purpose of helping others to follow a crucified Christ and to show that crucified living is the only way to truly grow in the humility of Christ.

To conclude this chapter, it is important to reemphasize the vital role that spiritual leadership plays in the church. Without it the church will not mature and grow in the fullness of Christ (EPHESIANS 4:11-13). However, the contrast between worldly leadership and spiritual leadership cannot be over emphasized. The world leads by authority regardless of the spiritual condition of the leaders. Jesus said, *"Not so with you. Instead, whoever wants to become great among you must be your servant, and whoever wants to be first must be your slave—just as the Son of Man did not come to be served but to serve and to give his life as a ransom for many"* (MATTHEW 20:26-28).

CONCLUSION

*T*he criticalness of humility to our relationship with God has been the main premise and purpose for this book. As we have discussed, pride is a spiritual cancer which blocks the mind and heart from the honest evaluation of the work and Word of God. The Pharisees refused to acknowledge the divine source of Jesus' miracles because of pride, their insatiable thirst for power, money, and respect, and thereby failed to see any value in the carpenter's son's teaching.

Without a humility carved out of an ever-deepening understanding of the truths we have discussed associated with the "nothingness" of Christ, we too will simply exist blinded in a physical world filled with evidence of so much more. Humility is our only solution to the devastating spiritual effects of pride. It is clear throughout the entire Bible that God opposes the proud; therefore, the understanding and development of humility must take top priority to sustain a vibrant relationship with God.

As I have tried to show, genuine humility expresses itself as much more than just a discreet calm temperament. A quiet controlled person can be just as prideful as a loud person. The Pharisees were often silent when Jesus taught because of Jesus' knowledge of the Scriptures and his acute ability at debating. The Pharisees hid their pride behind their quietness, religious clothing, and position. As in Jesus' time, the Word of God will always expose the prideful no matter how they cloth themselves or how faithful they might be to handed-down belief systems. Humility is the gateway to our understanding of God's truths which helps us to cut through our external religiosity and live open and free lives.

"Greatness" in the kingdom of God is never defined by position, prominence, or human success. Jesus made it clear that the first will be last and the last first. In other words, those who appear in this world to be wretched and poor, but have the "nothingness" or humility of Christ as their goal, are put at the front of the line spiritually. On the other hand, those who aspire for worldly success, who appear to be "first" and the "standard" will end being "last."

God is gracious in that he allows us to experience suffering, failure, disappointment, and loneliness with the hope that our pride will be broken, our need for God will become more evident, and humility will emerge as a state-of-being which will guide our hearts and the way we live.

POWER
IN
WEAKNESS

SECOND CORINTHIANS
& THE MINISTRY OF PAUL

MARTY WOOTEN

Available at www.ipibooks.com

Books from Illumination Publishers

Apologetics

Compelling Evidence for God and the Bible—Truth in an Age of Doubt, by Douglas Jacoby.

Field Manual for Christian Apologetics, by John M. Oakes.

Is There A God—Questions and Answers about Science and the Bible, by John M. Oakes.

Mormonism—What Do the Evidence and Testimony Reveal?, by John M. Oakes.

Reasons For Belief–A Handbook of Christian Evidence, by John M. Oakes.

That You May Believe—Reflections on Science and Jesus, by John Oakes/David Eastman.

The Resurrection: A Historical Analysis, by C. Foster Stanback.

True, Right, Better—A Defense of the Christian Worldview, by John M. Oakes.

When God Is Silent—The Problem of Human Suffering, by Douglas Jacoby.

Bible Basics

A Disciple's Handbook—Third Edition, Toney Mulhollan, Editor.

A Quick Overview of the Bible, by Douglas Jacoby.

Be Still, My Soul—A Practical Guide to a Deeper Relationship with God, by Sam Laing.

From Shadow to Reality—Relationship of the Old & New Testament, by John M. Oakes.

Getting the Most from the Bible, Second Edition, by G. Steve Kinnard.

Letters to New Disciples—Practical Advice for New Followers of Jesus, by Tom A. Jones.

The Baptized Life—The Lifelong Meaning of Immersion into Christ, by Tom A. Jones.

The Lion Never Sleeps—Preparing Those You Love for Satans Attacks, by Mike Taliaferro.

The New Christian's Field Guide, Joseph Dindinger, Editor.

Thirty Days at the Foot of the Cross, Tom and Sheila Jones, Editors.

Christian Living

According to Your Faith—The Awesome Power of Belief in God, by Richard Alawaye.

But What About Your Anger—A Biblical Guide to Managing Your Anger, by Lee Boger.

Caring Beyond the Margins—Understanding Homosexuality, by Guy Hammond.

Free Your Mind—40 Days to Greater Peace, Hope, and Joy, by Sam Laing.

Golden Rule Membership—What God Expects of Every Disciple, by John M. Oakes.

How to Defeat Temptation in Under 60 Seconds, by Guy Hammond.

Jesus and the Poor—Embracing the Ministry of Jesus, by G. Steve Kinnard.

How to Be a Missionary in Your Hometown, by Joel Nagel.

Letters from Jesus to the Seven Churches of Revelation, by Rolan Dia Monje.

Like a Tree Planted by Streams of Water—Personal Spiritual Growth, G. Steve Kinnard.

Love One Another—Importance & Power of Christian Relationships, by Gordon Ferguson.

One Another—Transformational Relationships, by Tom A. Jones and Steve Brown.

Prepared to Answer—Restoring Truth in An Age of Relativism, by Gordon Ferguson.

Repentance—A Cosmic Shift of Mind & Heart, by Edward J. Anton.

Strong in the Grace—Reclaiming the Heart of the Gospel, by Tom A. Jones.

The Guilty Soul's Guide to Grace—Freedom in Christ, by Sam Laing.

The Power of Discipling, by Gordon Ferguson.

The Prideful Soul's Guide to Humility, by Tom A. Jones and Michael Fontenot.

The Way of the Heart—Spiritual Living in a Legalistic World, by G. Steve Kinnard.

The Way of the Heart of Jesus—Prayer, Fasting, Bible Study, by G. Steve Kinnard.

All Available at www.ipibooks.com

Deeper Study

A Women's Ministry Handbook, by Jennifer Lambert and Kay McKean.
After The Storm—Hope & Healing From Ezra—Nehemiah, by Rolan Dia Monje.
Aliens and Strangers—The Life and Letters of Peter, by Brett Kreider.
Crossing the Line: Culture, Race, and Kingdom, by Michael Burns.
Daniel—Prophet to the Nations, by John M. Oakes.
Exodus—Making Israel's Journey Your Own, by Rolan Dia Monje.
Exodus—Night of Redemption, by Douglas Jacoby.
Finish Strong—The Message of Haggai, Zechariah, and Malachi, by Rolan Dia Monje.
In Remembrance of Me—Understanding the Lord's Supper, by Andrew C. Fleming.
In the Middle of It!—Tools to Help Preteen and Young Teens, by Jeff Rorabaugh.
Into the Psalms—Verses for the Heart, Music for the Soul, by Rolan Dia Monje.
King Jesus—A Survey of the Life of Jesus the Messiah, by G. Steve Kinnard.
Jesus Unequaled—An Exposition of Colossians, by G. Steve Kinnard.
Mornings in Matthew, by Tammy Fleming.
Passport to the Land of Enough—Revised Edition, by Joel Nagel.
Prophets I—The Voices of Yahweh, by G. Steve Kinnard.
Prophets II—The Prophets of the Assyrian Period, by G. Steve Kinnard.
Prophets III—The Prophets of the Babylonian and Persion Periods, by G. Steve Kinnard.
Return to Sender—When There's Nowhere Left to God but Home, by Guy Hammond.
Romans—The Heart Set Free, by Gordon Ferguson.
Revelation Revealed—Keys to Unlocking the Mysteries of Revelation, by Gordon Ferguson.
Spiritual Leadership for Women, Jeanie Shaw, Editor.
The Call of the Wise—An Introduction and Index of Proverbs, by G. Steve Kinnard.
The Cross of the Savior—From the Perspective of Jesus, by Mark Templer.
The Final Act—A Biblical Look at End-Time Prophecy, by G. Steve Kinnard.
The Gospel of Matthew—The Crowning of the King, by G. Steve Kinnard.
The Letters of James, Peter, John, Jude—Life to the Full, by Douglas Jacoby.
The Lion Has Roared—An Exposition of Amos, by Douglas Jacoby.
The Seven People Who Help You to Heaven, by Sam Laing.
The Spirit—Presense & Power, Sense & Nonsense, by Douglas Jacoby.
Thrive—Using Psalms to Help You Flourish, by Douglas Jacoby.
What Happens After We Die?, by Douglas Jacoby.
Wildfire—How Progressive Theology is Impacting the Church, by Daren Overstreet.
World Changers—The History of the Church in the Book of Acts, by Gordon Ferguson.

Marriage and Family

A Lifetime of Love—Building and Growing Your Marriage, by Al and Gloria Baird
Building Emotional Intimacy in Your Marriage, by Jeff and Florence Schachinger.
Hot and Holy—God's Plan for Exciting Sexual Intimacy in Marriage, by Sam Laing.
Faith and Finances, by Patrick Blair.
Friends & Lovers—Marriage as God Designed It, by Sam and Geri Laing.
Mighty Man of God—A Return to the Glory of Manhood, by Sam Laing.
Pure the Journey—A Radical Journey to a Pure Heart, by David and Robin Weidner.
Raising Awesome Kids—Being the Great Influence in Your Kids' Lives by Sam and Geri Laing.

Welcome
to the New

ILLUMINATION
PUBLISHERS
www.ipibooks.com

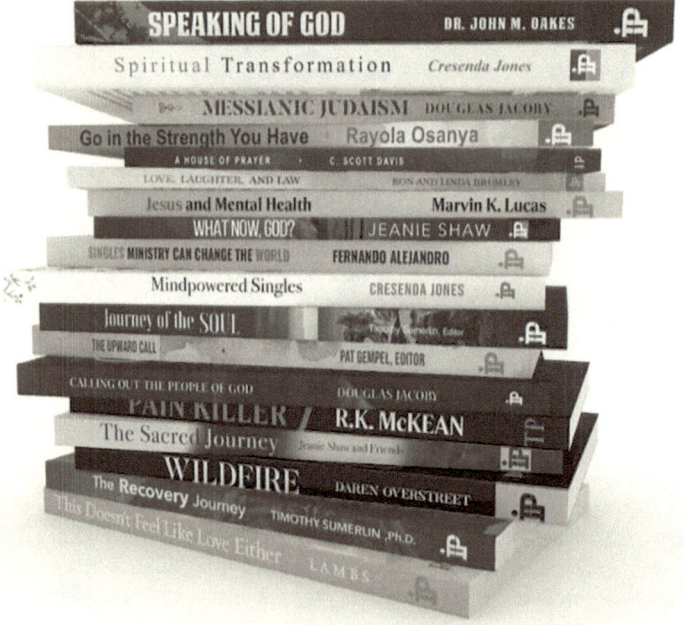

For additional books go to
www.ipibooks.com